NO LIMITS

Seven Keys to Life,
Legacy & Leadership

A.C. ROPER

No Limits

© 2025 by A.C.Roper

All rights reserved. No portion of this book may be reproduced, stored in a retrieval system, or transmitted by any means — electronic, mechanical, photocopy, recording, scanning or other — except for brief quotations in critical reviews or articles, without the prior written permission of the publisher.

The views expressed in this publication are those of the author and do not necessarily reflect the official policy or position of the Department of Defense or the U.S. government. The public release clearance of this publication by the Department of Defense does not imply Department of Defense endorsement or factual accuracy of the material.

ISBN: 978-1-962825-56-6

Atlas Elite Publishing Partners

Dedication

I dedicate this book with deep gratitude to my beloved wife, Edith. Your unwavering support, endless patience, and boundless love have been my greatest source of strength. This book is as much yours as it is mine. Your presence not only graces these stories but also vividly embodies the guiding principles within. In every sense, your influence continues to shape me into a better person. It is through your example that I am inspired to push the boundaries of what is possible and embrace the transformative power of purpose-driven living.

To my amazing daughters, Krystle and Amber, watching you grow into the incredible women you are today has been my greatest joy. Keep shining bright and never stop chasing your dreams. Always remember that you are the greatest legacy of my life.

I extend my deepest gratitude to my siblings, whose resilience and strength have been a beacon of hope throughout our challenging childhood. Your unwavering support and enduring spirit have been an inspiration, and this book is a testament to the remarkable fortitude we shared together. Our parents have passed away, but they would be proud to know that family bonds can overcome even the greatest of obstacles.

To the brave first responders and dedicated military personnel, your selfless service and unwavering commitment to protecting and serving our communities and our nation are the bedrock of our freedom and safety. Thank you for your courage and resilience.

My heartfelt dedication extends to friends and teammates who have supported me along this journey, and to my exceptional "Front Office Teams." Your steadfast dedication not only broadened my sphere of influence but also maximized my time, enriching me with wisdom and capabilities beyond imagination. Alongside extraordinary leaders and mentors, you have illuminated paths to hidden opportunities and untapped potential.

A special note of appreciation to Dr. Ellouise C. Johnson for your invaluable editing expertise and keen attention to detail. Your thoughtful insights and careful refinement have elevated this work, ensuring that its message is as impactful as it is clear. Thank you for your dedication to excellence.

At the core of it all stands my Heavenly Father, whose boundless love and grace have embraced and redeemed me from my transgressions through the immeasurable sacrifice of Jesus. His faithfulness is intricately woven into every aspect of my life, legacy, and leadership, and for that, I am forever grateful.

Table of Contents

Intro: Who Should Read This Book? 6

Prologue: In the Beginning 9

Chapter 1: Nurture Relationships 13

Chapter 2: Honor Humility 32

Chapter 3: Guard Integrity 53

Chapter 4: Practice Discipline 76

Chapter 5: Cultivate Excellence 103

Chapter 6: Build Partnerships 122

Chapter 7: Embrace Change 142

Epilogue: The Gift of Legacy 169

Endnotes 190

Author's Bio 196

Intro: Who Should Read This Book?

While many leadership principles are universal, this book expands the conversation by exploring leadership through the lens of life's broader purpose, deepening its impact and illuminating the true essence of legacy. In this publication, I remain steadfast in my lifelong commitment to effecting positive change and leaving a lasting impact on individuals and communities across a spectrum of contexts. Whether personal or professional spheres, public or private domains, or profit-driven and non-profit sectors, the insights presented in this book are geared toward those seeking to enrich lives, including their own. By offering genuine and credible leadership principles, this work serves as a guide to empowering individuals and organizations to attain remarkable and meaningful outcomes.

Each key chapter represents a fundamental aspect of personal growth and achievement, offering valuable insights and lessons that will shape the narrative of your life, legacy and leadership.

In the first chapter, you'll delve into the profound impact of cultivating meaningful connections with others. You'll discover how nurturing relationships not only enrich your life but also lay a strong foundation for personal growth. We'll explore three distinct categories of people and examine how each group has the potential to shape and influence your journey.

In the second chapter, you'll uncover the value of humility as a cornerstone of strong character. You'll explore how humility can transform personal development and influence the way you interact with the world. This chapter will also delve into your "position of perspective" and the importance of maintaining unofficial channels of communication, revealing how humility shapes these essential aspects of leadership and growth.

Chapter three clarifies the concept of integrity as the foundation of trust and respect. You'll discover the vital importance of aligning your life with your values and upholding unwavering moral principles. By doing so, you'll set yourself apart, understanding that true integrity is the foundation of authentic leadership and lasting relationships.

Chapter four introduces the "engine of discipline" as a powerful tool for achieving your goals and aspirations. You'll learn how self-control, coupled with the "cascading power of consistency," drives long-term success and helps you stay on course even when challenges arise.

In the fifth chapter, you'll delve into the pursuit of excellence and how mastering the ordinary paves the way for extraordinary success. You'll discover how striving for the highest standards can elevate your skills, enhance your work, and improve your overall quality of life.

The sixth chapter is focused on the power of collaboration and partnerships. You'll learn how synergistically working with others can drive innovation, foster growth, and achieve mutual success. However, politics can infiltrate and potentially derail these collaborative efforts thereby negatively impacting the effectiveness of group interactions.

In the seventh chapter, you will navigate the ever-evolving landscape of change with grace and resilience. You'll gain insights into the different types of change and explore the four responses to change, equipping yourself with essential skills for both personal and professional development.

In the epilogue, you will reflect on the significance of gifting a lasting impact to the world. You'll consider how your actions and choices throughout your tenure and various assignments will shape the legacy you leave behind, ensuring that your contributions resonate meaningfully throughout your lifetime and beyond.

And with that in mind, prepare to live a life with "No Limits!"

Let's begin.

Prologue: In the Beginning

"Don't despise these small beginnings, for the
Lord rejoices to see the work begin."

- Zechariah 4:10 (New Living Translation)

IN THE EARLY MORNING HOURS, long before the sun cast its warm glow across the sleepy streets of Birmingham, Alabama, a determined 21-year-old emerged from the warmth of his modest bed. Nestled within the confines of a public housing community, this young man possessed aspirations that set him apart from the ordinary. He was a financially poor college student with dreams that reached for the stars, but on this particular day, he knew that the dawn held a significance beyond measure. Today was the day that marked the commencement of an arduous journey into the heart of the Police Academy.

With a mixture of excitement and trepidation coursing through his veins, he prepared himself for the formidable task that lay ahead. An 80-mile drive loomed on the horizon, a daily ritual that would soon become his crucible. Weeks of relentless hardship awaited him: weeks brimming with sweat, tears, and the weighty burden of unrelenting stress. All of this was his initiation into an academy notorious for its unforgiving 50% graduation rate. It was a demanding path that would necessitate an unyielding resolve.

Each day, as the sun cast its first rays over the horizon, he embarked on that daunting 160-mile round trip, a grueling trek that tested his mettle. But he carried with him the knowledge that his journey was not one of solitude. No, it was fueled by his faith and the unwavering support of his family and the community that had cradled and nurtured him through the years. Their strength bolstered him, their hopes and dreams interwoven with his own.

Years later, the indomitable spirit of this tenacious youth would see him ascend to the position of Chief of Police, leading the largest police department in all of Alabama. It was a testament to the enduring power of community and determination—a symbol of what one can achieve with unwavering resolve and the steadfast support of those who believe in your potential.

But this story is not solely defined by its successes. It is a tapestry woven with multiple ambitions, each thread adding depth and complexity to the narrative. In the years preceding his journey into law enforcement, he etched three profound goals into the pages of his high school Memory Book. Becoming a Police Officer was merely the first brushstroke in the intricate masterpiece of his life's ambitions.

Beyond the precincts of policing, his second goal was to serve his country as an Army Soldier. This young man would later script history by becoming the first African American to rise to the esteemed rank of Lieutenant General in the U.S. Army Reserve. His journey took him from the bustling halls of the Pentagon to the commanding heights of Peterson Space Force Base in Colorado. There, he not only served as a sentinel, safeguarding North America against threats that transcended borders, but also as a steadfast symbol of dedication and leadership.

Yet, amidst the grandeur of these monumental achievements, he never lost sight of his third aspiration—a desire for love and companionship. Destiny intervened in the form of a blind date, an encounter that would forever change the course of his life. In Edith, the woman he met on that fateful evening, he found a love that would become the anchor of his life, steadfastly supporting him through the trials and triumphs of his extraordinary journey.

This story is a powerful reminder that each person carries a unique narrative, woven through twists and turns, challenges, and victories. As the author of your own story, it is imperative to remember the journey is an ever-evolving odyssey.

Every person has a story, and this is mine. Throughout the chapters of my life, I have nurtured and embraced seven foundational principles—my North Star—guiding me through life's complexities, shaping my legacy, and exemplifying unwavering leadership. These principles have been my steadfast companions, leading me through both the peaks and valleys of my journey. With deep conviction, I believe they hold the power to transform and enrich the narratives of others.

These chapters serve as a roadmap to what I believe is a life well-lived, offering wisdom and guidance to help you craft your own unique narrative. As you embark on this journey, remember that your story is still being written, and each chapter holds the potential for growth, fulfillment, and a legacy that endures.

In the pages that follow, you will journey through the intricate tapestry of my story, woven with its unique details and unexpected detours. Yet, this narrative is not mine alone—it is yours as well. Though each journey is distinct, there are shared experiences that make every sojourn a work of art. The threads of life's twists and turns—woven through challenges and victories—connect us in community. Our design may be dyed with difficulty, but it is also laced with the profound lessons that emerge from our deepest experiences.

As you turn these pages, I invite you to step into the role of the author of your own story. For this is not just a tale of my own experiences, but a reflection of the human journey, a story that we all participate in, each with our own unique chapters. Together, we will explore the profound notion that life should never reside on autopilot. Instead, it is a call to action, a reminder that our journey is an opportunity for course corrections, the acquisition of new skills, and the perpetual pursuit of personal growth.

Just as every book has a prologue that sets the stage for the story to come, let this prologue serve as an introduction to the grand narrative of life—a story in which you are not merely a reader, but an active participant. Your choices, actions, and decisions are the loom that weaves your tapestry, the compass that charts your course, and the ink that writes the next pages of your unique journey.

So, dear reader, I pose a question to you: What's your story? The time has arrived for you to grasp the pen firmly in your hand, poised and ready to inscribe the next extraordinary chapter of your life's journey. The blank pages that stretch before you are a canvas awaiting the imprint of your aspirations, your actions, and your unique vision. In this boundless expanse of possibilities, the power to shape your narrative rests firmly in your hands. So let's dig into these seven essentials with an open heart and a curious mind. Go ahead, dive into the chapters that await, knowing that the story of your life is still being written, for it is yours to create, yours to share, and yours to inspire.

Chapter 1: Nurture Relationships

> "To add value to others, one must first value others."[1]
>
> - John C. Maxwell

IN THE HEART OF BIRMINGHAM, Alabama, far from the bustling auto factories of Detroit where my parents had hoped to settle, my story took an unexpected turn. It all began when my father, A.C. Roper, a young man of the south who marched in the civil rights struggle, found his way up north in pursuit of employment in the auto industry. He eventually established roots in Detroit, but his heart remained tethered to his sweetheart, Shirley Williams back in Birmingham.

Their love story unfolded against the backdrop of a rapidly changing but troubling America of 1963. Earlier that year, George Wallace was sworn in as Governor of Alabama, declaring in his inaugural address, "Segregation now; segregation tomorrow; segregation forever." Against this backdrop, my parents fled the South, exchanged vows, and embarked on the journey of parenthood. The stage was set for my arrival in Detroit, Michigan—but fate had other plans. Around the sixth month of pregnancy, my parents decided to squeeze in a visit to Birmingham to see family before Detroit's harsh winter made road travel impossible. However, I had plans of my own and made my entrance into the world during that Birmingham visit—several months earlier than expected.

Unprepared for my early arrival, and with my dad needing to return to work in Detroit, my grandmother, a wise and loving figure, stepped in. She advised my parents to leave me in her care rather than face the challenges of a harsh Detroit winter without family support. The plan was for them to return for me in the summer when the weather improved.

Destiny had a different script. My grandmother, like so many who met me, instantly fell in love with the newborn I was. As my parents struggled to find their footing in long-term parenthood, I became the cherished child of 'Mom' as she was affectionately known. She was a force of nature—tough, disciplined, and the hardest-working person anyone had ever encountered. Foolishness, disrespect, and laziness were not tolerated in her presence.

Mom's entrepreneurial spirit led her to open the Cougar Lounge on Old Finley Avenue, a neighborhood cornerstone where everybody knew your name. Regulars and newcomers alike gathered there for camaraderie, a cold beer, and a hearty Cougar Burger. It wasn't the ideal place to raise children, but Mom made it work. Late at night, my brother and I would curl up in the corner booths, our feet dangling over the edges, just long enough to rest on folding chairs. We'd drift off to sleep to the tunes of the jukebox and the occasional burst of laughter from patrons celebrating the weekend.

What made this unconventional upbringing truly special were the familial relationships forged within those four walls. Mom knew everyone who walked through the Cougar Lounge's door, both professionally and personally. She was not just the owner, manager, bartender, and server; she was a friend, counselor, mentor, helper, and sometimes even a bouncer. She had an uncanny knack for discerning who needed a kind word, a free meal, or a few dollars to help them through tough times. Relationships mattered deeply to her.

As the oldest grandchild, I shared a unique bond with her. She relied on me to hold the fort when she was away, and she became my role model, teaching me the art of nurturing relationships. The Cougar Lounge was more than just a bar—it was a place where community thrived, where strangers became friends, and where the power of meaningful connection was on full display. Those formative years left an indelible mark on my soul... Nurture Relationships.

Nurture has many definitions, but most coalesce around feeding, and protecting. Others speak to supporting and encouraging as during the period of training or development; or to foster.

As a leader we are often required to judge, assess, or evaluate leaders or even potential leaders prior to delegating responsibilities, assignments or even selecting for promotions.

How these candidates relate to people and nurture relationships must be a major criterion for consideration. Recently, I was part of one of these discussions and used an analogy. Let me forewarn you—alongside my forty-plus-year military career, I also spent over three decades in law enforcement. To the chagrin of my family, friends, and co-workers, my analogies often draw from these experiences. It's much like a pastoral friend of mine who played collegiate and professional football—naturally, his analogies tend to lean toward sports.

While discussing a leadership issue, I remarked that this leader would get the job done and accomplish the mission—but there might be a crime scene left in their wake. I painted a vivid picture of a workplace littered with 'dead bodies,' yellow crime scene tape blocking certain rooms, and the leader standing there proudly proclaiming, "We met our goals!" Yet behind them lies a trail of broken relationships, hurt feelings, and mistrust. Even if objectives are achieved, sustaining success in a toxic environment is nearly impossible. People and relationships must truly matter. It's never a good sign when a mission is accomplished, but CSI (Crime Scene Investigations) must be called in for the cleanup. Unfortunately, I've seen this scenario play out time and time again, even in high-performing organizations.

Those who lead well can accomplish the mission without the mess. The 'sweet spot' of leadership is a delicate equilibrium where the complex dynamics of a team or organization align in perfect harmony. It is the ideal point of convergence where a leader masterfully balances achieving objectives, fostering accountability, and nurturing meaningful relationships.

At the heart of this equilibrium lies the art of goal accomplishment. Effective leaders are adept at setting clear, achievable objectives and steering their teams toward their realization. They provide the vision, direction, and resources necessary for success. However, this achievement-oriented aspect of leadership is just one facet.

Simultaneously, accountability is upheld as a fundamental pillar. A leader ensures that individuals within the team are responsible for their respective tasks and deliverables. Accountability is not about micromanagement but rather about creating an environment where team members feel a sense of ownership over their work and its outcomes.

Yet, amidst these objectives and accountabilities, lies the nurturing of relationships. Exceptional leaders understand that people are not mere cogs in a machine but unique individuals with their aspirations, challenges, and motivations. They invest time and effort in building trust, fostering open communication, and creating a culture of collaboration and camaraderie.

This 'sweet spot' is where team members are not just colleagues but true collaborators who are willing to go the extra mile because they feel valued and inspired. It's where goals are achieved, not through coercion, but through shared commitment and dedication. It's where accountability isn't punitive but seen as a means of personal and collective growth.

In summary, the 'sweet spot' in leadership is a testament to the delicate art of balance. It's where leaders orchestrate the symphony of goal accomplishment, accountability, and relationship-building to create an environment where success flourishes, and individuals thrive. Achieving this balance requires not only skill but also empathy, adaptability, and a genuine commitment to the growth and well-being of both the organization and its people.

If we remember every person has potential, we will value our daily interactions much more. It's an unfortunate reality but we often judge people based on where they are today and fail to consider their value tomorrow. We must look beyond the 'now' and consider what the person can be!

It brings to mind a personal experience from my early days as a young officer assigned to the Police Academy as a full-time instructor. One would assume that recognition and appreciation are inherent in any learning environment, especially in an academy dedicated to guiding young citizens through rigorous training and development while transforming them into public servants committed to a cause greater than themselves. Right? Unfortunately, that wasn't the case for me...

Motivating Memories

There are some moments in life that stand out and serve as a 'motivating memory.' Motivating memories keep you going and give you that extra kick when times are tough. The reason some people don't understand your 'grind' is because they don't have your motivating memories. Let me share one regarding potential.

One day I had a bright idea (some would say that's rare) so I went to my supervisor (who will remain nameless) and advised him I wanted to learn more about leadership so I could teach and become some type of an expert. It's been over thirty years but I still remember how he, simply put, burst out in uncontrollable laughter. I mean a belly shaking, tears rolling down his face type of laughter. Through the chuckles he managed to breathlessly whisper, "You?" As if to ask, surely not you. I fully recognize the deck was stacked against me since I was the youngest member of the team in both age and experience, and the only African American on the academy staff. The issue was not what I was or where I was but who I could become.

What if he had nurtured a relationship which would have afforded him the opportunity to go deeper rather than judge me based on what he saw or perceived on that day? From that foundation, he could have then asked probing questions, like why is that important to you? What can he do to help me accomplish my dream? But instead, he laughed. I left that department a year or so later for a much better opportunity closer to home but yet I never forgot my dream or the sting of his laughter.

That supervisor would probably be stunned in silence to know I am continuing to fulfill that leadership dream. He would likely be further taken aback to know that I have served in a multitude of executive leadership positions, mentored other successful leaders and have lectured nationally and internationally on strategic leadership topics. On the other hand, he might simply say he saw it in me the whole time (eye roll). By the way, I had the honor of returning to that department a few years ago to conduct a strategic leadership session for the police and fire department executive leadership teams.

Though a 'motivating memory,' this story also highlights a fundamental truth: the company we keep is a decision of profound significance that can shape our future in both subtle and transformative ways. We inevitably become reflections of those we choose to surround ourselves with thereby making making this dynamic instrumental in shaping the course of our lives.

Within the realm of relationships, there are three distinct categories of people, each with the potential to influence our journey in unique ways:

1. Dream-breakers: These are the individuals who, regrettably, harbor disbelief, skepticism, or negativity. They are the skeptics who cast doubt on your ambitions and, at times, even on the faith you have in yourself and your potential. Engaging with dream-breakers can be akin to navigating a minefield of negativity. The energy spent trying to convince them of your aspirations can drain your vitality and erode your self-confidence. In essence, they hold the power to diminish your sense of purpose if you allow them. It is imperative to recognize that you need not give anyone the authority to derail your dreams.

2. Dream-makers: These extraordinary individuals are like guardian angels who enter our lives to support and elevate our pursuits. They may be mentors, role models, or peers who genuinely believe in your vision and offer unwavering encouragement. The presence of dream-makers is like a steady breeze beneath your wings, lifting you forward as you strive toward your goals.

Cultivating relationships with these individuals is invaluable, as they provide guidance, inspiration, and a sincere desire to see you succeed. They understand that your success is not a threat to their own but rather a testament to the power of collaboration and shared dreams.

3. Dream-stakers: I must admit I created this category. So, while it may not be commonly discussed, it represents a unique group of individuals who, in their own way, depend on our success. These are individuals who may not hold malicious intent but whose aspirations and dreams are deeply intertwined with your success. They recognize that your achievement can catalyze their own, or they rely on your prosperity to secure their own future. While not inherently negative, it is essential to discern whether these relationships are symbiotic or parasitic. In healthy partnerships, the aspirations of both parties are uplifted by mutual support. However, if the relationship becomes one-sided, where your dreams are consistently sacrificed for the sake of others, it's essential to reevaluate the balance.

> **In healthy partnerships, the aspirations of both parties are uplifted by mutual support.**

This is really about value propositions in assessing how a relationship's qualities, experiences, and interactions contribute to your personal and professional development. In summary:

* Dream-breakers deduct from and deny the value of your dream.

* Dream-makers deposit into and help determine the value of your dream.

* Dream-stakers discern from and define the value of your dream.

In the grand mosaic of life, the power of association cannot be understated. It's a reflection of the wisdom found in the adage, "Show me your friends, and I'll show you your future." The individuals with whom we choose to share our journey can either buoy our spirits providing a chorus of support and motivation, or they can act as anchors holding us back with their doubts and negativity.

As we navigate the intricate tapestry of relationships, it is incumbent upon us to be discerning stewards of our own aspirations. To reach our highest potential, we must gravitate toward dream-makers, those who uplift and inspire us, and endeavor to reciprocate their support. Simultaneously, we must acknowledge the existence of dream-breakers and exercise the wisdom to preserve our purpose and vitality by limiting our exposure to their negativity. And finally, we must foster healthy dream-staker relationships, ensuring that mutual benefit and shared dreams remain at the core of our connections.

In essence, the people we surround ourselves with become more than mere companions; they become architects of our destinies. The choices we make in the realm of companionship can propel us toward our dreams or weigh us down with doubt. Ultimately, the power rests with us to cultivate relationships that nurture our aspirations and contribute positively to the grand tapestry of our lives.

Although my supervisor didn't recognize it, there is potential in everyone and legacy leaders help tease it out. They nurture relationships and understand that productivity increases when people are encouraged. Leaders should not view people as just a role or function on the org (organization) chart. They are people with families, hopes, goals and dreams. When leaders nurture relationships, they foster greater productivity and commitment. When parents do the same, they build deeper trust and transparency with their children.

Another word for nurturing in the context of relationships is investing. Whether it's stocks, bonds, retirement accounts, or any other financial tool, we easily understand that investing means giving up or depositing money in the near term for a (hopefully) greater payoff in the future. In the world of finance, merely breaking even is not considered success.

The same principles apply to nurturing relationships. We have to purposefully deposit energy, time and even money in the near term with the hopes of meaningful relationships in the long term. In this technological age, the value of our investing is evidenced by our cell phones, calendars and credit cards (for most of us, the cell phone contains our calendar and method of payment as well).

The cell phone reveals our communication patterns via calls or texts. The calendar reveals where and with whom we spend our time and the credit card or other method of electronic payment informs us where we spend our money.

This means your cell phone reveals who is important to you because it reflects where you focus your communication. Your calendar proves who and what matters most because it shows where you invest your time. And finally, your credit card statements declare your priorities because they reveal where you spend your treasure (money).

Returning to the earlier crime scene analogy, a CSI team would run forensics, examine the evidence, and draw conclusions about how you manage relationships. This analogy applies to business, but even more so to our familial relationships. After all, it would be a tragedy to win the world but lose your home.

At your retirement party, the anecdotes shared might indeed revolve around impressive sales records or remarkable metrics achieved during your career. While these accolades are undoubtedly a testament to your skills and dedication, they possess a somewhat ephemeral quality. They are akin to shooting stars, blazing brightly for a moment before making way for the next "hotshot" on the horizon.

Sales records and metrics, however remarkable, are not etched in stone. They are markers of your achievements at a specific point in time and are subject to change with evolving markets, technology, and competition. This transient nature can make them somewhat illusory as a measure of one's lasting impact.

Furthermore, the relentless pursuit of such metrics, while it may bring short-term gains, can potentially be costly in the long run. The unrelenting drive to outperform oneself and others can lead to burnout, strained relationships, and a narrow focus on immediate results at the expense of long-term sustainability.

The true legacy you leave behind is not solely defined by these metrics but by the intangible, enduring impressions you've made on colleagues, clients, and the organization itself. It's the mentorship you provided to junior team members, the collaborative spirit you fostered, and the culture of respect and integrity you helped cultivate. These are the aspects that endure, shaping the organization's ethos long after you've retired.

In essence, while sales records and metrics have their place in recognizing achievement, they are just one facet of a multifaceted career. The stories told about your contributions should reflect not only your professional accomplishments but also the lasting mark you've left on the people and the culture of the organization. These are the stories that truly resonate and endure. Ultimately, we are reminded that a successful career is not measured solely by numbers but by the positive and lasting impact we have on those around us.

A Leadership Laboratory

It's vitally important to start building and nurturing relationships from the onset. No where is this more profound than the U.S. military. For background, I began wearing an Army uniform at the age of 13 in the 9th grade of high school after joining the Junior ROTC (Reserve Officers Training Corp) program. I was then "early commissioned" at the age of 19 as a 2nd Lieutenant. I still say I was much too young to be thrust into that type of leadership position. However, I found the Army to be an excellent leadership laboratory because it provides a structured environment where individuals can develop and refine their leadership skills through practical experience and training. I clearly admit I have some biases but here's my rationale:

Hierarchy and Structure:

The Army has a clear hierarchical structure with levels of authority and responsibility. This allows individuals to progress through different leadership roles from entry-level positions to commanding units. Valuable experience is gained at each level.

Diverse Teams:

Soldiers come from diverse backgrounds, cultures, and experiences. Leading teams with such diversity helps individuals learn to adapt their leadership styles to effectively manage and motivate a wide range of personalities and skill sets.

Training and Education:

The Army invests heavily in leadership training and education programs, such as Officer Candidate School and Non-Commissioned Officer Professional Development courses. These programs provide both theoretical knowledge and practical exercises to develop leadership skills.

Real-world Challenges:

Army personnel often face real-world challenges, such as decision-making under pressure, teamwork in high-stress situations, and adapting to rapidly changing circumstances. These experiences are invaluable for developing leadership resilience and adaptability.

Ethical and Moral Development:

Army leaders are expected to uphold the highest ethical and moral standards. With a strong emphasis on character development, they learn the importance of integrity, responsibility, and accountability in leadership.

Mentorship:

Army leaders often serve as mentors to junior personnel, guiding and coaching them along their journey. This mentorship provides valuable role modeling and insights that are essential for leadership development.

Feedback and Evaluation:

Regular performance evaluations and feedback mechanisms help individuals identify their strengths and areas for improvement as leaders, fostering continuous growth.

Leadership in Adversity:

The Army often operates in challenging and adverse conditions, teaching leaders how to make tough decisions and lead in demanding situations.

This leadership laboratory offers a unique environment where individuals can learn, practice, and refine their leadership skills. This is especially true in the Army Reserve, where most Soldiers have dual careers. Successfully managing both while maintaining a healthy family life requires balance, teamwork, and collaboration.

Unlike the National Guard, which is state based, the Army Reserve is a federal, community-based force with approximately 175,000 Soldiers and over 12,000 civilian employees operating across all 50 states, five territories, and more than 30 countries. It serves as a critical force provider of trained, ready units and Soldiers essential for the Army to fight and win wars while also responding to homeland emergencies on behalf of the American people.

I recall my assignment to serve a tour as the Deputy Chief of the Army Reserve at the Pentagon. In this role, my focus was twofold. Primarily, I was responsible for developing strategy and policy, as well as planning, programming, and resourcing at the National, Departmental, and Service levels. Additionally, I was responsible for coordinating, integrating, and synchronizing our Army Reserve Staff within the Headquarters Department of the Army. The key was executing the Chief's vision by integrating Army Reserve force capabilities in support of the nation while ensuring we set the conditions for long-term success.

I mention this background because the Pentagon is the world's largest office building; consequently, where bureaucracy can easily run amok in deeply entrenched processes, metrics, position papers, and briefings. Fortunately, my veteran staff understood the importance of relationships. Soon after I came on board, they compiled a list of key individuals I should meet beyond the standard business interactions. This was no small task as the building is exceptionally busy (I call it grinding). Coordinating schedules and finding available time slots was challenging, but they got it done.

Over several days, I marched from office to office, shaking hands, introducing myself, and intentionally building relationships beyond briefings, board meetings, and periodic updates.

Interestingly, I found a unique connection with each person, one that extended beyond the typical work product. For example, in one civilian's office, I spotted a "yellow brick" in his bookcase. It piqued my interest since I also have a yellow brick, and I know those are given to graduates of the FBI National Academy in Quantico, VA after running the Yellow Brick Road. That was a connection point. In one General's office, I discovered he was a fellow Christian so at the end of our meeting we prayed for each other. I could share story after story but to sum it up, those connections are personal but also have professional benefits as I soon learned that most of the important business is conducted outside of the primary meeting. In simple terms, the primary meeting will officialize previous agreements made in the hallway or at lunch.

We must delve deeper into the importance of nurturing relationships, specifically exploring how these connections foster both personal and professional growth.

Imagine relationships as an intricate web that interconnects people's lives and experiences. Just as a spider weaves its web with precision, we too must carefully weave the delicate strands of trust, empathy, and genuine connection. These strands are not merely fragile threads; they have the potential to become the sturdy ropes that support us in times of need.

In today's fast-paced world where instant messaging and virtual meetings dominate, it's easy to overlook the significance of face-to-face interactions. However, true relationships are often solidified through shared experiences and genuine conversations. While technology can facilitate communication, it's the personal touch that fosters understanding, empathy, and trust.

Consider a simple example: a manager who takes the time to know their team members on a personal level, understands their strengths and weaknesses, and acknowledges their aspirations. This manager doesn't just see employees as cogs in the organizational machine but as individuals with unique qualities and dreams. Such leaders are more likely to inspire loyalty, dedication, and a sense of belonging among their team members.

Moreover, when leaders prioritize relationships, they create a culture of collaboration and innovation. Team members feel comfortable sharing ideas and taking calculated risks because they know their contributions are valued. This collaborative environment can lead to breakthroughs, improved problem-solving, and overall better performance.

In your personal life, nurturing relationships can also have a profound impact. By investing time in your family, you build a foundation of trust and support that can weather life's storms. These relationships are the bedrock of emotional well-being, providing a sense of belonging, love, and security.

Returning to the Pentagon experience, those personal connections made in the hallways and during lunches weren't just casual encounters. They were the building blocks of trust and collaboration. When individuals find common ground beyond their professional roles, they are more likely to go the extra mile to support each other's goals.

These relationships extend beyond the workplace as well. A simple connection like the shared experience of the "yellow brick" from the FBI National Academy can lead to lasting friendships and collaborations outside of the office. These personal bonds create a network of trust that can be tapped into for advice, support, and collaboration in various aspects of life.

In summary, nurturing relationships is more than just a soft skill—it is a strategic advantage with immense significance in both personal and professional spheres. It is the profound art of recognizing the untapped potential within every individual—a power that, when harnessed, can lead to remarkable outcomes.

More than anything, it is a deliberate investment in the bonds that connect us, affirming the belief that the true currency of life lies in trust, loyalty, and the mutual growth that flourishes from meaningful connections.

In the professional world, these relationships become the cornerstone of success. They foster collaboration, promote effective communication, and encourage a culture of shared goals and values within teams and organizations. Furthermore, they act as conduits for opportunities, as people naturally gravitate toward those they trust and respect. In this arena, nurturing relationships isn't merely a pleasant attribute; it's the bedrock of career advancement and long-term success.

On a personal level, the significance of nurturing relationships is equally profound. It enriches our lives with the warmth of camaraderie, provides a support system during challenging times, and enhances our overall well-being. It's through these connections that we grow, both as individuals and as members of a broader community.

In the grand tapestry of life, our legacy isn't solely woven from the threads of our achievements. Instead, it is defined by the lasting impact we've had on others—the indelible marks we leave through the relationships we nurture along the way. It's the stories people share about how we inspired, supported, or uplifted them. It's the knowledge that, through our commitment to meaningful connections, we've not only achieved personal success but also made the world a better place, one relationship at a time.

In essence, nurturing relationships is the ultimate investment in the currency of humanity. It is a timeless and invaluable strategic advantage that transcends industries and borders, reverberating through generations to create a legacy beyond our own lifetimes. As we continue to cultivate these connections, we sow the seeds of empathy, understanding, and cooperation, enriching the human experience for those who follow in our footsteps.

To ensure the dividends continue to flourish, leaving a legacy that extends far beyond our years… **Nurture Relationships.**

Reflective Questions for Chapter 1

Relationships are the foundation of effective leadership and personal fulfillment. Whether they are professional alliances or personal connections, strong relationships are built on trust, communication, and shared purpose. As you reflect on this chapter, consider the following questions to evaluate the health of your relationships. Are you nurturing these bonds with intention and sincerity? How are you investing in the people around you to create a network of support and collaboration that will stand the test of time?

1. How do I currently balance my focus between achieving goals and nurturing relationships in my personal and professional life?

   - Reflect on how well you are balancing task-oriented success with meaningful connections and where you might adjust to improve.

2. Who in my life acts as a dream-breaker, dream-maker, or dream-staker, and how do these relationships affect my progress toward my goals?

   - Consider the roles people play in your life and whether their influence is helping or hindering your personal and professional growth.

3. What are some practical ways I can invest more time, energy, and resources into nurturing relationships with those who matter most to me?

   - Look at your communication patterns (phone, calendar, spending habits) to see if they reflect the priorities in your relationships.

4. Can I recall a 'motivating memory' where someone supported or challenged my potential, and how has it shaped the way I nurture relationships with others today?

   - Reflect on past experiences, either positive or negative, that have influenced your approach to connecting with others.

5. What steps can I take to leave a legacy of trust, collaboration, and respect in my relationships both at work and at home?

   - Consider how you want to be remembered by others and how you can begin building that legacy now through your interactions and relationships.

Chapter 2: Honor Humility

"Humility is not thinking less of yourself, it's thinking of yourself less."[2]

- Rick Warren

AS I REFLECT ON THE concept of humility, my mind wanders back to a particular incident from my early days as the Birmingham Chief of Police. It was a challenging time marked by escalating crime rates and a strained relationship between law enforcement and the community.

One evening, I attended a town hall meeting where community members voiced their grievances and concerns. As I took the stage, I could feel the weight of my position and the expectations placed upon me to have all the answers. My initial instinct was to assert my authority and project an image of unwavering confidence. But a voice inside me told me to approach the situation differently.

Instead of launching into a rehearsed speech or attempting to showcase my expertise, I humbly began by acknowledging the pain and frustration the community was experiencing. I shared that I didn't have all the solutions, but I was committed to listening and working together to find a way forward. I invited community members to share their thoughts and ideas, emphasizing that their perspectives were invaluable in shaping the future of law enforcement in our city.

To my surprise, the atmosphere in the room shifted. The initial tension began to dissolve as people felt heard and valued. Individuals who were initially hesitant to speak up now bravely stepped forward to share their experiences and suggestions. I listened intently, taking in their stories, and seeing the situation from their perspective. Through humility, I had unlocked a powerful tool – the power of empathy. In retrospect, this sense of empathy wasn't foreign to me since my youngest brother, Shawn, was senselessly murdered at the age of 19 in Birmingham and my wife, Edith, had also lost a brother to violence in the city.

Over the following weeks, I continued to engage with the community, actively seeking input from diverse voices and incorporating their ideas into our approach to crime prevention and community policing. This inclusive approach transformed the dynamics between the police department and the citizens we served. The sense of "us versus them" was gradually replaced with a sense of unity and collaboration. Crime rates began to decline and in fact, we achieved historic lows. In addition, the trust between law enforcement and the community started to grow stronger.

The experience taught me a profound lesson about humility as a leader. It wasn't about pretending to have all the answers or always being the smartest person in the room. True humility was about recognizing the collective wisdom of the community and empowering others to contribute their unique perspectives. It required putting aside my ego and the need to prove myself, and instead, focusing on the greater good and fostering an environment of trust and mutual respect. Humility, often considered the crown jewel among virtues, is indeed one of the most misunderstood and paradoxical qualities in human character. It stands as a virtue that defies simple categorization, for it is neither mere submission nor a complete lack of confidence, ambition, or pride. Instead, humility encompasses a delicate balance of these characteristics while embodying a profound understanding of one's place in the world.

At first glance, many perceive humility as a state of "submission" where individuals acquiesce to others' will and suppress their own voices. However, true humility is far from being a doormat. It is the ability to yield when appropriate, recognizing the wisdom in listening to others and valuing diverse perspectives. It's about knowing when to lead and when to follow, not out of insecurity, but with wisdom and empathy.

Another common misconception about humility is that it equates to a "lack of confidence" or ambition. Nothing could be further from the truth. Humility does not diminish self-confidence; rather, it strengthens it. A humble individual possesses a quiet, inner assurance that enables them to pursue their goals with determination while remaining receptive to feedback and open to growth. They understand that there is always room for improvement and that they do not have all the answers.

Furthermore, humility does not entail a "lack of pride" in one's achievements or identity. Instead, it involves a healthy form of pride, one grounded in gratitude and self-awareness. Humble individuals can take pride in their accomplishments and attributes without diminishing the worth of others. Their pride is not rooted in comparison or the need to be superior but in a deep appreciation for their unique journey and the contributions they can make to the world.

So, what is humility, if not a mere negation of these traits? Humility can be succinctly defined as the freedom from excessive pride or arrogance. It is the ability to recognize one's strengths and weaknesses with clarity and honesty, to value the worth of every individual, and to approach life with a sense of wonder and curiosity.

Merriam-Webster defines arrogance as "an attitude of superiority manifested in an overbearing manner or in presumptuous claims or assumptions,"[3] whereas pride is often defined as "an inordinate amount of self-esteem or conceit."[4]

Indeed, the distinction between arrogance and pride is subtle yet significant, as it hinges on how one perceives oneself and interacts with others. Webster's definitions aptly capture the essence of these two concepts.

Arrogance, as defined, entails an attitude of superiority, often accompanied by an overbearing manner. It is marked by an inflated sense of one's own importance or abilities, often at the expense of others. Arrogant individuals tend to make presumptuous claims and assumptions, frequently underestimating or dismissing the perspectives and contributions of those around them. This attitude can be off-putting and hinders effective collaboration and communication.

Arrogance often stems from a deep-seated need for validation or a fear of vulnerability, leading individuals to adopt an overconfident facade that masks their insecurities.

Unfortunately, this sense of arrogance has invaded national politics where serving the Constitution and people of the United States is often secondary to "winning" partisan battles at all costs.

On the other hand, pride is often described as having a high regard for oneself, but it's not necessarily negative. Pride, in moderation, reflects a healthy sense of self-esteem and self-worth. It's the recognition and appreciation of one's achievements, qualities, and identity. Pride can be a driving force for personal growth and motivation, spurring individuals to set and achieve ambitious goals. When expressed in a balanced way, pride can be a source of confidence and self-assuredness, which can be inspiring to others.

The difference between arrogance and pride is a matter of balance and self-awareness. While pride can be a positive force when grounded in humility and gratitude, arrogance arises when that sense of self-worth becomes overbearing and is expressed at the expense of others. Recognizing this distinction is crucial for fostering healthy relationships, effective teamwork, and personal growth.

However, the key lies in moderation. When pride becomes excessive or inordinate, it can transform into "hubris," a state of excessive pride or self-confidence that often leads to a sense of invincibility. This is where pride takes a perilous turn and starts resembling arrogance. Hubristic individuals may overestimate their abilities, ignore advice or feedback, and display an overbearing attitude that alienates others.

Just in my lifetime, hubris the perilous trait of excessive pride and self-confidence, has left a trail of cautionary tales throughout history and across various spheres of leadership. It's a phenomenon that has been personified in far too many leaders who, despite their tremendous performance and potential, tragically succumbed to the belief that they were beyond the ethical boundaries and rules governing their organizations.

One of the most glaring examples of hubris in leadership can be found in the corporate world. Consider the case of Enron, once a prestigious energy company, and its CEO, Jeffrey Skilling. Under Skilling's leadership, Enron appeared to be an unstoppable force, consistently reporting record-breaking profits. However, beneath this veneer of success, a culture of deceit and arrogance thrived. Top executives manipulated financial statements, concealing massive debt and inflating earnings. When the truth was exposed, Enron's downfall became one of the most infamous corporate scandals in history, causing widespread financial ruin and massive job losses.[5]

In the political arena, the tale of hubris is not uncommon. Leaders who become intoxicated with power and believe they are impervious to the principles of democracy and ethics often face dire consequences. A striking example is the downfall of Richard Nixon during the Watergate scandal.[6] As the President of the United States, Nixon's overconfidence and disregard for the rules of law led him to engage in covert actions to maintain his grip on power. This hubris ultimately led to his resignation, marking a significant moment in American history.

Even in the realm of sports, hubris can tarnish the legacy of remarkable athletes. Like many others, I watched in amazement as Lance Armstrong, a celebrated cyclist who won the Tour de France multiple times, fell from grace when it was revealed that he had been using performance-enhancing drugs. His initial denials and media reports of audacious efforts to silence accusers exemplify a classic case of hubris.[7] Armstrong's eventual confession not only cost him his titles but also damaged his reputation irreparably.

These examples underscore the devastating consequences of hubris in leadership. It blinds individuals to their own moral compass, leading them to disregard the principles of integrity, transparency, and accountability. Leaders who succumb to hubris often prioritize short-term gains and personal interests over the long-term health and sustainability of their organizations or careers. It erodes trust, not only in the leaders themselves but also in the institutions they represent. The trust between leaders and their teams, stakeholders, and the public is all adversely affected. Rebuilding this trust can be a herculean task, often requiring a change in leadership and a steadfast commitment to ethical reform.

The examples of Enron, Richard Nixon, Lance Armstrong, and many others serve as stark reminders that even the most accomplished leaders, those with exceptional performance and potential, are not immune to the destructive influence of hubris. Unfortunately, I've witnessed this toxic trait emerge in remarkably talented military leaders who began to see themselves as above the rules and policies of the Department of Defense.

I am Third

During my fifth-grade year, I vividly recall immersing myself in Gayle Sayers' captivating autobiography, *I am Third*.[8] For those who may not be familiar or came into this world after his remarkable feats, let me offer some insight. Gayle Sayers, a legendary figure in college and NFL history, holds the distinguished honor of being enshrined in both the College and Pro Football Halls of Fame. Within the pages of his autobiography, he eloquently articulated a profound philosophy: God is first and holds the paramount position in his life, followed second by the cherished bonds he shares with his family and friends, and then he himself humbly occupied third place. This profound revelation about his priorities in life played a pivotal role in laying the foundation for his extraordinary achievements.

To aspire to great heights, like Mr. Sayers, one must possess a considerable degree of self-confidence and self-esteem. However, maintaining emotional equilibrium requires cultivating confidence beyond oneself. When this balance falters, arrogance and excessive pride tend to emerge, disrupting relationships and teamwork.

Those who mismanage this balance become difficult collaborators, often draining the energy from a room or team. Hopefully, while avoiding the pitfalls of becoming one ourselves, we've all encountered such personalities. Their conviction extends to an extreme belief that every project's fate rests solely on their shoulders and that every achievement is exclusively their own. Naturally, this also means that any recognition or praise is, in their eyes, meant solely for their glory.

A profound realization dawned on me long ago; success is never a solo project or solitary journey but a collaborative endeavor. This epiphany solidified its place in my consciousness during various phases of my career. It crystallized during my tenure as Chief of Staff at my Army Reserve Headquarters, deepened as I assumed the role of Chief Operating Officer at my church, and reached its zenith when I took on the mantle of Chief of Police in my hometown. In each of these diverse arenas, I was privileged to lead alongside an extraordinary, brilliantly talented team, whose collective wisdom often eclipsed my own.

My operating philosophy was quite simple and that was to provide the guidance so each supporting team could use their experience, talents and skills to operate within my intent. In the military, we refer to this leadership philosophy as "Mission Command" which prioritizes decentralized decision-making and the empowerment of subordinate leaders. Leaders are often amazed at the results when people are given the freedom to operate, create solutions and solve problems without every detail being micromanaged. However, as the leader, we can delegate authority but not responsibility because ultimately we are still responsible for the outcomes: the good, the bad and the ugly!

As I reflect on the importance of humility today, I see it as a powerful force capable of transforming individuals, teams, and communities. It is the glue that binds people together, fostering trust, respect, and understanding. Through humility, I have witnessed the emergence of creative solutions, the breaking down of barriers, and the formation of meaningful connections. Indeed, humility is not a sign of weakness but a testament to the strength and wisdom of a true leader. It is a virtue that shapes character, guides decision-making, and influences the trajectory of our lives. As I continue on my journey, I carry with me the understanding that humility isn't just a word or a concept — it is a way of being that can lead us to profound personal growth and create a positive impact on the world around us.

Humility is critical because arrogance and pride destroy trust, an essential foundation for life, legacy, and leadership. It's often said that trust is the currency of relationships. I wholeheartedly agree, but I also submit that nothing erodes trust faster than arrogance and conceit.

So, how do we put this principle into action and avoid these pitfalls? The key is recognizing the value, gifts, talents, and skills that others bring to the team or assignment. Some leaders say, "Well, they know I appreciate them." But do they? Appreciation must be demonstrated, not assumed. I advocate for intentional action, where a leader does or says something tangible, leaving no room for doubt in the mind of a family member, co-worker, or partner.

Through numerous assignments and projects as a leader in public safety and the military, I developed a tag line when receiving an orientation or an information brief. I would tell the other person, who was often lower ranking but highly proficient in their field, "Make me smart in this area." They would typically chuckle or respond with something like, "Sir, I've been doing this for 15 years." Their response always opened the door for me to counter with,

"Wow, you must really be good. Just share some of your knowledge with me so I can understand this better."

Quite often I could see them get more comfortable, stand a little taller, and strut their stuff as they explained the intricacies of some project or metric. I can only imagine the conversation when they returned to their desk and told their co-workers the General didn't know anything about this project but I squared him away.

Another interesting tidbit for leaders is to share their opinion last. This is not always possible depending on the urgency of a decision. Absent a time crunch, allow the team to discuss and bounce it around because quite often, once the leader weighs in with an opinion, the free flow and creativity grinds to a screeching halt. Why? Because very few people will choose to disagree with the boss publicly. However, they will leave the room and whisper about the Boss' goofy idea.

Referring to the balance I mentioned earlier, I am not suggesting that you abandon self-confidence or adopt a defeatist attitude, that would simply mean the pendulum has swung too far in the opposite direction. Every person has value, but humility means also recognizing and appreciating the value in others.

As individuals ascend the ranks and reach higher echelons of success within an organization, an unfortunate reality often unfolds: the higher they climb, the more obscured their view becomes of the day-to-day realities at ground level. This phenomenon is especially pronounced in centralized organizations, where the layers of hierarchy are more pronounced, and the gap between leadership and frontline operations widens significantly.

The concept of "managing by walking around" is a strategy frequently advocated for by leaders who seek to maintain a connection with their organization's grassroots. During my tour as the

Deputy Commander (DCOM) of U.S. Northern Command, the military's combatant command charged with defending the United States and Canada, my front office staff printed two 7x5 cards for my daily binder. One was my daily schedule and the other was my circulation card which focused on three key areas. This card listed my key recurring (peer level or higher) leadership engagements, my upcoming external travel dates and locations, and my internal visits to the various headquarter elements. These visits were my "walking around" engagements and with a headquarters the size of ours it was important to list out the various joint directorates and special staff sections and actually program the visits in a pragmatic manner. It gave me the opportunity to check in, take a few questions and maybe present a DCOM coin for excellence to some deserving teammate.

However, even with this approach, we as leaders are constrained by the limitations of time and physical distance. While we may stroll through the offices or visit different branches, the breadth and depth of an organization can be overwhelming. In the vast terrain of a multinational corporation or a sprawling bureaucracy, one leader can only cover so much ground, and only during limited windows of time.

Leaders must compensate for limitations of time and physical distance.

Heard it through the Grapevine

This intriguing conundrum underscores a fundamental truth in the realm of organizational dynamics—the indispensable role of unofficial channels of communication in complementing the official chain of command. While the official hierarchy provides structure, clarity, and a defined flow of information, it is the unofficial channels that breathe life into the organization, facilitating the nuanced exchange of ideas, insights, and concerns.

Digging deeper, here's why these unofficial lines of communication are indispensable:

Real-time Information:

In dynamic environments, especially those where swift decision-making is imperative, relying solely on the official chain of command can be impractical. Unofficial channels often provide a direct and real-time conduit for information to flow from the frontline to the leadership. This ensures that critical issues, emerging challenges, and innovative ideas reach decision-makers promptly.

Perspective and Context:

The insights garnered from unofficial channels can offer a more nuanced understanding of ground-level operations. Leaders who engage with employees directly or encourage open feedback mechanisms gain access to valuable context that might not be apparent from a distance. This additional perspective enables leaders to make more informed decisions and formulate strategies that align with the realities on the ground.

Employee Engagement:

Encouraging unofficial lines of communication fosters a culture of engagement and trust. When employees feel that their voices are heard and that they can communicate directly with leadership, they are more likely to feel valued and motivated. This, in turn, can lead to increased job satisfaction and productivity.

Issue Resolution:

Many challenges and conflicts within an organization can be resolved swiftly and effectively through informal communication channels. When employees have the means to address concerns directly with leaders or peers, problems can be nipped in the bud before they escalate into larger issues that disrupt operations.

Innovation and Adaptation:

Unofficial lines of communication often serve as conduits for innovative ideas and suggestions. Employees on the frontlines are well-positioned to identify opportunities for improvement or to propose creative solutions to existing problems. By tapping into these sources, organizations can remain agile and adapt to changing circumstances.

In practice, fostering unofficial lines of communication involves creating an organizational culture that encourages openness, transparency, and accessibility. It means actively seeking feedback, conducting regular town hall meetings, and providing platforms for employees to share their insights and concerns. It also entails leadership's commitment to listening, responding, and acting upon the information received from these channels.

The bottom line is as leaders ascend the ladder of success, they must acknowledge the inherent challenges in maintaining an accurate understanding of ground-level realities. Decentralized organizations exacerbate this issue. While I champion "managing by walking around" as a valuable practice, it has its limitations. To bridge the gap effectively, organizations must cultivate and nurture unofficial lines of communication. These channels not only provide a lifeline to the grassroots but also enhance decision-making, foster employee engagement, and facilitate innovation, ultimately contributing to the organization's long-term success and resilience.

However, it's essential to recognize that while unofficial channels can be a powerful force for positive change, they also come with potential pitfalls. Informal communication can sometimes lead to misunderstandings or the spread of inaccurate information.

Therefore, embracing both channels, by striking a balance between official and unofficial, enables organizations to navigate the complexities of today's fast-paced world with agility and adaptability while maintaining a strong foundation of trust and collaboration. It is within this delicate balance that the true potential of communication within an organization is realized.

As Birmingham's Chief of Police, I adopted a remarkably enlightening practice, personally attending patrol precinct roll calls across our city's diverse communities. These decentralized precincts, each led by a dedicated Captain, represented the most visible and grassroots level of city government, operating around the clock to ensure the safety and security of our neighborhoods.

My experiences during these visits were both insightful and rewarding. Dressed in my patrol uniform, I relished the opportunity to engage with our officers, providing them with real-time updates and answering their questions. These interactions were far from scripted. They were unvetted, unfiltered, and brimming with the raw authenticity that emerges when frontline professionals speak their minds.

The questions posed by our officers ran the gamut, and I embraced each one with a sense of purpose. Some queries I could address on the spot, drawing from my experience and knowledge, while others necessitated follow-up with my staff. What became abundantly clear to me was the striking resemblance between our Police

Officers and the Soldiers in the Army—they shared a commitment to delivering the unvarnished truth about their work conditions, the level of community support they received, or the efficacy of various work initiatives we were implementing.

Yet amidst these candid exchanges, I encountered a fascinating yet somewhat disconcerting phenomenon. It became evident that the executive messages we meticulously crafted at the top of the hierarchy often underwent a transformation as they traveled down the chain of command, passing through what I could only describe as "ranks of distortion." By the time these messages reached the end-users, the officers on the frontline, their content had morphed into something entirely different, unfamiliar, and even perplexing.

This peculiar journey of information underscored the paramount importance of effective leadership communication. It illuminated the critical need for clear, transparent, and unambiguous messaging within our organization. It also reinforced the notion that leadership is not just about making decisions at the top but ensuring that these decisions are comprehended and faithfully executed throughout the ranks. Ultimately, that was my responsibility.

> **Regardless of size and scope, every organization has a critical need for clear, transparent, and unambiguous communication.**

In the upcoming chapters, I will delve deeper into the intricacies of leadership communication, exploring strategies and practices that bridge the gap between intent and interpretation. Through this, we can work toward building a more coherent and aligned organization, one where messages from the executive level resonate authentically at every level, ultimately fostering a culture of clarity, trust, and effective leadership.

Essentially, these visits afforded me, as the CEO, the opportunity to demonstrate my willingness to listen, ask questions, probe deeper, and read body language, all in an effort to truly understand the why, much more than the how. This is just one technique for humble leaders to gain a sense of reality beyond PowerPoints, metrics, and sales reports.

Max Depree, Author of *Leadership is an Art*, famously said, "The first responsibility of a leader is to define reality."[9]

Let that sink in...

As I peel back the onion, this is a powerful assertion which implies there are leaders of families and organizations operating in a different reality or an alternate universe! For my comic book fans, it's akin to "Bizarro World," a fictional planet in the *Superman* comics, created as a mirror image or "opposite" of the familiar DC Comics universe inhabited by Superman and other superheroes.[10] It's essentially a bizarre and twisted version of Earth where everything is reversed, leading to often comical and nonsensical situations. I referenced "Bizarro World" so often in my police conference room that one day, a senior Captain walked into my office and gifted me a small bust of Bizarro Superman. Since then, that bust has had a place in each of my offices.

Leaders who fail to define reality and neglect to cultivate unofficial lines of communication often find that their perceptions, priorities, and decision-making processes diverge significantly from the commonly understood shared reality. These leaders might appear disconnected from the everyday challenges and concerns faced by the majority. They may make decisions that baffle or even harm those they lead because their perspective and priorities seem rooted in a different dimension altogether, their own versions of Bizarro World.

Humble leaders understand that valuable insights can come from anyone. By remaining receptive to diverse perspectives and leveraging unofficial lines of communication, they gain a deeper understanding of the realities and challenges their teams face. By identifying and leveraging these strengths, organizations can achieve better outcomes and solve problems more effectively. It is critically important for leaders to discover their own strengths and those of their team members to improve overall performance and satisfaction.

Position of Perspective

People with humility are approachable, open, and willing to listen. This allows them to lead their families or organizations from a "position of perspective," something often lacking in the arrogant and conceited.

The term "position of perspective" isn't widely recognized, but I use it to describe the vantage point from which an individual observes, interprets, or analyzes a situation, idea, or event. It represents the specific standpoint a person adopts when considering a matter, significantly shaping their perception and understanding.

Leaders who are disconnected or hold a false view of reality are the ones who fail. Their mission is derailed, their team distracted, and their organization dis-eased due to what I call problems "lying in wait."

These leaders are often blind to the negative undercurrents flowing just beneath the surface of their family or organization. When the surface finally cracks and a fissure erupts, the geyser explodes, and people are left wondering, "How did that happen?"

To illustrate the profound impact of humility in leadership, let's explore real-life examples from various fields. These cases will not only highlight the power of humility but also reveal the dangers of arrogance.

From a historical perspective, consider Mahatma Gandhi, a figure renowned for his humility.[11] His approachability and willingness to listen made him a powerful leader during the Indian independence movement. His ability to empathize with the masses and understand their struggles allowed him to lead from a position of deep perspective, ultimately leading to the liberation of a nation.

In contrast, the historical figure of Emperor Nero serves as a cautionary tale of arrogance and disconnection. Nero's self-centered rule and detachment from the suffering of his people eventually led to his downfall and the disintegration of the Roman Empire.[12]

In the corporate world, humility has proven to be a key ingredient for success as evidenced by the example of Satya Nadella, CEO of Microsoft and CNN's 2023 Business CEO of the Year. Nadella's leadership style is defined by humility, which has enabled him to foster innovation and collaboration within the company.[13] Under his guidance, Microsoft experienced a remarkable resurgence.

On the flip side, we have the cautionary tale of Elizabeth Holmes, the founder and former CEO of Theranos. Reportedly, her overconfidence and refusal to listen to dissenting voices led to a scandal of epic proportions, resulting in legal troubles, a prison sentence, and the downfall of her company.[14]

Within families, humility plays a pivotal role in maintaining harmony and cohesion. Consider parents who lead their families with humility. They actively listen to their children's concerns, respect their opinions, and acknowledge their own fallibility. These parents create an environment where open communication and mutual respect thrive, strengthening the family unit.

In contrast, domineering and arrogant family leaders stifle open dialogue, causing resentment and estrangement among family members. Such leaders may be blindsided by the simmering discontent within their family until it erupts into irreparable conflicts.

In the realm of organizations, humility can be the difference between success and failure. Take the case of Johnson & Johnson during the Tylenol crisis in the 1980s. James Burke, the company's CEO at the time, demonstrated remarkable humility and responsibility by recalling over 31 million bottles of Tylenol following a tampering incident. His swift and decisive action not only saved lives but also preserved the company's reputation.[15]

On the other hand, leaders who are disconnected from reality and blind to the negative undercurrents within their organizations can lead them into a downward spiral. WorldCom, once a prominent telecommunications giant, collapsed due to leadership arrogance and a lack of transparency, ultimately resulting in one of the most significant corporate scandals in history.[16]

In all these examples, humility emerges as a defining trait of successful leaders. It enables them to connect with people, understand their needs, and lead with empathy and authenticity. Humble leaders have the capacity to recognize their own limitations and seek input from others, creating an atmosphere of trust and collaboration.

Conversely, arrogant leaders often fail to see the warning signs, and the problems 'lying in wait.' They remain oblivious to the discontent simmering beneath the surface until a crisis erupts, leaving their followers wondering how such a catastrophe could occur.

The examples drawn from history, corporate leadership, family dynamics, and organizational management underscore the enduring value of humility in leadership while also highlighting the perils of arrogance and disconnection. For those who aspire to lead effectively, embracing humility should be a paramount goal, as it serves as the compass guiding them through even the most challenging leadership landscapes.

In conclusion, humility is not a sign of weakness but a wellspring of strength. It empowers leaders to lead from a position of perspective—making informed decisions, fostering collaboration, and ultimately achieving lasting success. Humility allows leaders to embrace the complexity of the human experience, recognizing that true power lies not in dominance but in the ability to connect, learn, and grow.

Although often overlooked and minimized by modern society, humility is a virtue that, when cultivated, fosters harmonious relationships, effective leadership, and a deep sense of purpose. So, as you journey through life, **Honor Humility.**

Reflective Questions for Chapter 2

Humility is a powerful yet often misunderstood trait. It's not about downplaying your strengths, but about recognizing the contributions of others and being open to learning and growth. Are you leading with an attitude of service and gratitude? Use these questions to explore how you can remain grounded, seek feedback, and embrace the perspectives of those around you, regardless of your position or level of expertise.

1. How do I currently demonstrate humility in my personal and professional interactions, and where might I be confusing humility with weakness or a lack of confidence?

- Reflect on your understanding of humility and identify areas where embracing it could strengthen your relationships and effectiveness.

2. Can I recall a situation where arrogance or excessive pride may have hindered my ability to lead or collaborate effectively? What lessons can I learn from that experience?

- Consider past instances where a lack of humility impacted outcomes and how adopting a humble approach might have led to a better result.

3. Who are the individuals in my life that exemplify humble leadership, and what specific qualities do they possess that I can incorporate into my own behavior?

- Think about role models who lead with humility and how their actions inspire trust and collaboration.

4. In what ways can I actively seek and value the perspectives and contributions of others to lead from a "position of perspective?"

- Plan actionable steps to become more approachable and open-minded, intentionally enhancing your understanding of others' viewpoints.

5. How can I cultivate humility to build trust and leave a positive legacy in both my personal relationships and professional endeavors?

- Reflect on the long-term impact of humility on your legacy and identify daily practices that honor humility in your interactions.

Chapter 3: Guard Integrity

> "The greatest asset, even in this country, is not oil and gas. It's integrity. Everyone is searching for it, asking, 'Who can I do business with that I can trust?'"[17]
>
> *- George Foreman*

IN THE YEAR 2018, HOLDING the rank of Major General, I embarked on a profound journey to the hallowed grounds of France. There, I had the honor of leading the distinguished Army Reserve delegation as we gathered to solemnly commemorate the centennial of World War I's culmination. This catastrophic global conflict unfolded its harrowing chapters from 1914 to 1918 and embroiled over thirty nations in its tumultuous grip. It reshaped the world order and had enduring consequences on the 20th century. As we reflected on the sacrifices made during those years, it was striking to recognize that the storied lineage of many active-duty Army infantry units endures to this day within the ranks of the U.S. Army Reserve.

The organizational perspective held immense significance, but there was the deeply personal thread of reflection that wove through the tapestry of that war. My reflections invariably gravitated toward the indomitable spirit of my grandfather, Corporal William Roper, a proud Buffalo Soldier who in service with the

366th Infantry Regiment, embarked for the battlefields of France. His mission: to fight for freedoms he himself was denied on home soil. It was a sacrifice laden with significance emblematic of the unwavering dedication that defined the thousands who, like him, served honorably despite the adversities they faced at home.

During my visit, I had the profound privilege of treading the very ground where my grandfather had contributed his courage to the Meuse-Argonne Campaign. Amidst the drizzle of that poignant day, as I traversed those historic fields, my thoughts inevitably turned to a contemplation of the past. I wondered, "What words of wisdom might Granddad have shared about his grandson rising to the rank of General?" Yet beyond personal achievement, the question that truly resonated was, "What would Granddad think of an Army that had given his grandson the opportunity to ascend to such heights, an Army that had evolved to reflect the ideals of freedom and equality he so valiantly defended?"

Granddad's legacy was memorialized in his service records. It wasn't about the awards he received or the honors and recognition he was denied due to the color of his skin. Instead, his legacy was summed up in two simple words.

You see, I have a copy of his discharge papers. Where it evaluated his service for character, it simply stated: "Character: Excellent."

Two words that mean so much. Two words that speak to integrity, moral courage, and personal standards.

Why so? You have to think back to World War I and the state of our country. You must remember at that time in America, Blacks were treated as second class citizens and denied the rights and basic freedoms guaranteed in our Constitution, including the right to vote.

Certainly, it's undeniably ironic and strikingly hypocritical when we consider the situation where individuals without personal freedom are dispatched to foreign lands to sacrifice their lives in the pursuit of others' freedom. Our history is marred by instances where Black soldiers, despite facing segregation, mistrust, and being assigned menial duties, displayed unwavering commitment to die for a country they still believed in. This poignant paradox highlights the complex and contradictory nature of the struggles for freedom and equality that have defined our nation's history.

These Soldiers like Corporal Freddie Stowers, 371st Infantry, 93rd Division who led his company on an attack in France to eliminate a heavily entrenched German position on a hill. "Faced with incredible enemy resistance, Corporal Stowers took charge, setting such a courageous example of personal bravery and leadership that he inspired his men to follow him in the attack."[18] Stowers was severely wounded, but continued to fight until he succumbed to his wounds and died. He gave his life on that hill on September 28, 1918. Nearly 73 years later, on April 24, 1991, he was posthumously awarded the Medal Of Honor. Two of his surviving sisters accepted the award which was presented to them by President George H.W. Bush. Corporal Stowers was denied his recognition in life but honored in death. I have a personal photo of me standing at his grave on a stormy day in France and rendering a hand salute in grateful appreciation for his sacrifice for our nation. Soldiers like him paved the way for Soldiers like me.

Character: Excellent

In society, the primary focus is on performance, but legacy leaders understand integrity is of greater importance because what a person "is" gives meaning to all that he "does." As we often say, our video has to match the audio. Who are you and what do you stand for? Integrity and character are still important. Integrity and character define us as individuals and our organizations.

In society, the primary focus is on performance, but integrity is of much greater value and importance.

> **In society, the primary focus is on performance, but legacy leaders understand integrity is of greater importance.**

The *Cambridge Dictionary* defines integrity as the quality of being honest and having strong moral principles that you refuse to change[19] whereas character is the particular combination of qualities in a person or place that makes them different from others.[20] In fact, the root word for integrity is "integer" which is a whole or complete number. This type of legacy leadership focuses on the whole life and not just the public sphere. It's an unfortunate reality that leaders who walk in integrity stand out, look different and are often swimming upstream against the current values and culture of society.

Leadership is a profound journey that demands unwavering commitment and a profound sense of responsibility. At their core, leaders are the guiding stars, the "true north" of their organizations, providing not just direction but also the moral compass that shapes the collective actions of their teams. This role transcends the professional realm; it delves deep into the realm of character and leader development, a responsibility that cannot be delegated or outsourced.

The foundation of this responsibility rests on a leader's presence, both physical and emotional. A leader's physical presence ensures they are accessible and approachable to their team. It fosters open lines of communication, making it easier for issues to surface and for guidance to be provided.

Equally important is emotional presence, which involves being attuned to the well-being of team members. A leader who is empathetic and understanding creates an environment where trust and psychological safety thrive.

Character development lies at the heart of this responsibility. Leaders must serve as exemplars of the values and principles that underpin their organization's culture. It is through their own actions, ethics, and integrity that these values are exemplified, instilling them as the core of the organizational DNA. In this way, leaders become the living embodiment of the ideals they wish to see flourish within their teams.

Leader development is another facet of this duty. Leaders must not only invest in their own growth but also in nurturing the leadership potential of those they lead. This involves mentorship, coaching, and providing opportunities for skill enhancement and growth. By doing so, leaders ensure a legacy of leadership that endures beyond their own tenure. Air Force General Glen VanHerck, Commanding General of the North American Aerospace Defense Command (NORAD) and U.S. Northern Command (USNORTHCOM) would often say, "The number one job of a leader is growing other leaders." After serving and watching him for three years, I can say he believed it and lived it.

The most important job of a leader is growing other leaders!

In sum, this profound responsibility should never be underestimated. Leaders are the architects of organizational culture, and their commitment to character and leader development sets the tone for the entire organization. It is a responsibility that begins with their own unwavering commitment to the proper values and extends to the development of those they lead, ensuring that the principles of excellence and integrity continue to flourish, making a lasting impact on the organization's present and future.

Kouzes and Posner, authors of *Credibility* explain that:

> *Honesty is absolutely essential to leadership. If people are going to follow someone willingly, whether into battle or into the boardroom, they first want to assure themselves that the person is worthy of their trust. They want to know that the would-be leader is truthful, ethical, and principled.*[21]

Leaders serve as the unwavering compass that guides their organization's course. They bear the profound responsibility of cultivating character and leadership excellence. This crucial duty is not a task that can be delegated or outsourced to others; it rests squarely on the shoulders of those who lead. It begins with a leader's unwavering presence and commitment, which serve as the crucible through which the organization's core values are meticulously forged and deeply embedded. In essence, leaders are the living embodiment of the principles and ideals that should permeate every facet of their organization.

An Ethical Drumbeat

As I learned with the Birmingham Police Department, leaders must maintain a constant ethical drum beat. As I was preparing to take the Chief's helm, I made several organizational promises and one was to personally teach the academy ethics class to every new recruit class. There were times we had to adjust the recruit training schedule so I could fulfill that mandate. As I often explained to other Police Chiefs who were surprised at my actions, it was important for me to set the ethical foundation in the beginning. Integrity matters! Character counts!

Oh, our values on the letterhead and mementos were "Serving with Ethics, Effort, and Excellence" but nothing spoke to ethics like the Police Chief personally dedicating 4 hours a session to teaching integrity and character. Why? Because those values serve as the building block for trust, and no organization can succeed when there's a trust deficit. If the organization begins to act inconsistent with its values it will lose the trust of those who rely on it.

Les T. Csorba, former White House Advisor for Presidential Personnel and author of *Trust,* succinctly links trust as a foundational principle to leadership:

> *Leadership is built on many characteristics such as humility, service, vision, courage, and so on, but, fundamentally, leadership is built on trust. You cannot sit on a broken chair. Neither can a leader lead without sitting on a seat of trust.*[22]

We often talk about the "trust bank" in relation to police-community relations. The analogy is similar to having a savings account at a local bank, where every police-citizen interaction is either a deposit into the trust account or a withdrawal. This means every vehicle stop, every criminal report, and every arrest matters. While I'm not aware of any specific scientific research, I've often wondered, how many deposits does it take to make up for a withdrawal?

Studies show a reduction in police calls for service after a high-profile use-of-force incident. This suggests that communities turn away from calling 911, seeking alternative means of resolution, often leading to acts of revenge and retaliatory shootings. In response, these departments must then embark on the slow and tedious task of rebuilding trust, one citizen at a time.

Some argue that modern-day law enforcement is in the midst of an "ethical crisis," and this crisis of trust affects everything: recruiting, retention, service, and daily interactions. I often spoke about how the challenged communities that needed us the most trusted us the least. Who would have thought the day would come when we would put body cameras on police officers?

Let there be no mistake about it. I am a huge proponent of body cameras and even rolled out the largest body camera program in the state of Alabama, but it still speaks to a crisis of trust.

In this age of social media, instant news, and police body cameras, trust remains the currency of relationships. As the most technologically connected society in human history, trust has become the most sought-after commodity in both business and interpersonal relationships.

The greater the trust, the stronger the relationships. This accelerates exchanges, saving time, and as we know, time is money. However, the lower the trust, the weaker the bond, resulting in additional expenditures of time, money, and effort.

Trust is the most sought-after commodity in both business and interpersonal relationships.

Likewise, trust facilitates both personal and organizational transactions, while a lack of trust can hinder, delay, and even destroy success. Trust isn't free; it is costly and must be earned day by day. It is difficult to build but easily destroyed.

Misconduct erodes the very fabric of trust. We must live and work by a higher standard. Unfortunately, trust has steadily declined across every sector of society. Scandals have touched business, sports, media, politics, and more.

In fact, the two professions to which I have dedicated my life are not exempt. In law enforcement, allegations of excessive force, racial profiling, and police militarization have shaken the foundation of police-community relations. The military has also faced ethical challenges, including sexual harassment and assault, senior leader misconduct, and academic cheating at our most prestigious academies.

During my ten-year tenure as Birmingham Police Chief, one of the most arduous chapters unfolded in the form of an excessive force case. It was a formidable test of integrity and leadership, a moment when I stood at a crossroads, torn between my unwavering commitment to our department's policies and the daunting task of testifying against my own officers in a civil suit. As I reflect upon those trying times, I cannot deny the restless nights that plagued me, the countless prayers I whispered in search of guidance, and the weight of the responsibility that rested squarely on my shoulders. But when the moment arrived, and I took my place in the witness box, I knew I had to be resolute in upholding my convictions.

The trial became a crucible of character, where I faced not only the legal proceedings but also the court of public opinion. The journey was anything but easy; it was a tumultuous, uphill battle. I often felt isolated, like a lone figure navigating treacherous waters. The sideways glances and hushed whispers were a constant reminder of the difficult path I had chosen.

However, in that critical moment, I understood my solemn duty to be the true north for our Police Department and our community. I had to stand as a beacon of unrelenting commitment to our principles and policies, especially when the currents of doubt and adversity threatened to pull me under.

It was a test of leadership, one that demanded steadfastness and moral courage. The headline in the opinion section of *The Birmingham News* boldly proclaimed, "With excessive force testimony staring him down, Birmingham Police Chief Roper doesn't blink." This assertion underscored the resilience required to lead with integrity and uphold the principles upon which our department and society depend.

Interestingly, the Editorial Board explained the very principles I'm advocating by writing,

> *The chief's testimony should in no way be viewed as siding with the suspect over his own officers. But knowing that many would jump to that conclusion, Roper gave his testimony anyway.*
>
> *Doing the right thing is easy when the crowd is with you. Integrity is when you're willing to do the right thing, even when you know you're going to take some lumps for it.*
>
> *In a world where integrity is increasingly not recognized, much less valued, we salute Chief Roper.*[23]

While this incident and its aftermath received widespread publicity, I find greater satisfaction in the everyday choices and behaviors that remained within the confines of my office and conference room. On numerous occasions, I defended my officers and their "Use of Force," understanding the chaotic, volatile and uncertain situations. These situations arose daily and required split-second decisions with life-or-death consequences. Yet in some instances, I declined to testify in court proceedings where a politician hoped my reputation of integrity would influence a judge or jury. Such occurrences often involved some of the most prominent leaders in the state, who found themselves facing criminal or civil actions and believed my support could sway the jury in their favor.

Too often, it's easy to blur the lines and fade the black and white into gray, creating a space where no clear ethical mandate exists. But this inevitably leads to lower standards. Trust me when I say, when you set a lower standard, you also set a lower expectation!

One common challenge is the misconception that ethical standards are solely a leadership issue. In reality, everyone plays a role in setting and enforcing the proper ethical climate. We must eliminate the "bystander mentality," where co-workers recognize character issues but choose to look the other way.

These character deficiencies develop early but are often only identified from below. Leaders remain blind to them, and we've all seen cases where individuals lacking integrity are promoted into supervisory roles.

For leaders, organizational integrity means ensuring that our organizations, divisions, and staff know what to do and do it. Integrity, often defined as the quality of being honest and having strong moral principles, is a multifaceted virtue that transcends the notion of simply doing what's right when no one is watching. It's a concept that has intrigued and inspired individuals across cultures and generations. The prevailing idea that integrity comes to the forefront only when we believe ourselves to be in isolation belies the profound nature of this virtue. From my own journey, I've come to appreciate that the true essence of integrity resides in how we conduct ourselves in every circumstance, particularly when we are in the company of others.

At its core, integrity represents a commitment to a set of values and principles that guide our actions and decisions. It's not merely a matter of personal virtue but a reflection of our character that extends into the public sphere. The solitude test of integrity, where one's behavior remains virtuous when unobserved, is certainly a valuable litmus test of one's moral compass. However, it's an incomplete assessment of this intricate quality.

In the presence of others, the significance of integrity is magnified. This is where the rubber meets the road, as our choices and actions have a tangible impact on the lives and perceptions of those around us. The measure of integrity isn't just about doing the right thing; it's about doing the right thing even when it's challenging, inconvenient, or unpopular. It's about consistency, authenticity, and a willingness to uphold our principles, not because it's easy but because it's the right thing to do.

Consider the individual who, when alone, might easily succumb to shortcuts, deception, or ethical compromises. In isolation, they may appear to lack integrity. However, when placed in a social context, their true character emerges. Do they stand by their values, even if it means facing adversity or standing against the prevailing tide? Or do they succumb to peer pressure, compromise their principles, and betray the trust of others?

Integrity is the unwavering thread that weaves our private and public personas into a cohesive whole. It's a testament to our authenticity and reliability. It is the moral foundation upon which trust, respect, and meaningful relationships are built. When we consistently uphold our values and principles, whether alone or among peers, we not only fortify our own character but also inspire and influence those around us. Our integrity becomes a source of guidance and motivation for others, setting a standard for ethical behavior in the collective spaces we inhabit.

> **Integrity is the unwavering thread that weaves our private and public personas into a cohesive whole.**

Integrity is not some solitary virtue confined to moments of isolation; it is a dynamic and far-reaching aspect of our character that shines brightest in the company of others. It is the persistent commitment to our principles, the moral compass that guides our decisions, and the measure of our authenticity. By embracing integrity as a guiding force in all circumstances, we not only shape our own character but also contribute positively to the world and inspire others to walk the path of virtue and honor.

In my extensive involvement in investigations and inquiries, I have witnessed numerous instances of ethical misconduct occurring in plain view of citizens, co-workers, and supervisors, even when individuals were aware they were being recorded by cameras. These situations reinforce the idea that integrity is not confined to moments of solitude; rather, it is a quality that should shine brightest in the full spectrum of human interactions. Integrity is about consistently upholding ethical standards, regardless of who may or may not be watching. It is about remaining committed to principled conduct even in the face of temptations or pressures to compromise those principles.

In essence, integrity is a measure of our character, revealed not just in the absence of an audience but also in our firm dedication to ethical behavior when our actions are under scrutiny. It is a vital attribute that should guide our actions and decisions in all circumstances, fostering trust and respect within our communities and workplaces.

To combat the erosion of trust, we must be increasingly self-critical and reflective. However, even self-checks have their limits. We must determine our true north or ethical boundaries before the storm. It's not much different than building a house. You dig the foundation before the rain saturates the ground. Once the storm strikes, it's much too late to start digging a foundation and building a structure. Likewise, we must establish our ethical foundation before facing a moral dilemma. It's not about being perfect because we all make mistakes but in leadership our lifestyle has an impact on our message. To develop and protect your integrity, start by identifying your core values. These are the values most important to you. These are the values where compromise is not an option, no matter what.

We sometimes need help examining our own motives, behaviors and actions. We need a continuous feedback loop. Organizationally we need 360-degree evaluations by peers. Why? Because everyone puts their best foot forward when their supervisor is present. In Chapter 6, when discussing partnerships, I highlight the value of a support team.

Well, one key member of that team must be a confidant who you can tell everything. I mean a person that you can look in the eye and tell the good, the bad and the ugly! These confidants must also have the green light to look you in the eye and give you the unvarnished truth without fear or repercussion. These personal road guards are invaluable, but unfortunately, too many leaders lack the humility to submit themselves to the critical eye of another. This pride leads to blind spots.

I believe we've all been disappointed when "giants fall." I am referring to the people we have admired, whether from near or afar, who were swept away by major ethical failures. It is especially disheartening when a leader serves as a role model or has the responsibility of correcting others yet lives the same lifestyle as those warranting correction. I am speaking of senior officers who slammed the gavel on their subordinates while committing the same offenses.

How does this happen? How do the public persona and personal lifestyle drift so far apart? I had to confront these questions, having lived my adult life in three roles: Soldier, Officer, and Minister. Deep within my core, I believed I could uphold the same integrity in each environment, allowing for seamless transitions. It was important for me, as it is for you, to build a sense of alignment where integrity is woven into every aspect of our lives.

Looking back, it wasn't difficult since I had drawn an ethical line in the sand. There are always invitations and temptations but they come with a heavy price that most regret at the end of the day. For example, leaders with personal rule sets would relax them on TDY (temporary duty) trips out of town. Hotels and bars became "ungoverned space." Locations where the stress and responsibilities of home would fade away during those few days of freedom. Work hard during the day and let the drinking, partying, and other foolishness rule the night. Many, many careers came to a crashing end due to the arrests, sexual harassment and assault complaints and "conduct unbecoming" investigations. Regardless of the uniform color, it occurred in the military and in law enforcement. With that being said, I must throw up a warning flag — these ethical lapses occur over time. In other words, there's a gradual erosion of ethical behavior over a length of time. Much more than not, ethical misconduct begins with the "little stuff" and then slides down a slippery slope.

I vividly remember our annual Army senior leaders' "Stewards of the Profession" Forums. These off-site gatherings were a time for us to confront the harsh realities and destructive behaviors that were undermining the very fabric of our teams and fighting formations. We delved into issues such as sexual harassment and assault, as well as the alarming rates of suicide, issues that not only shattered individual lives but also threatened to erode the unity and cohesion that form the bedrock of our military's effectiveness.

Despite our collective experience and the resources at our disposal, I must confess that I found it deeply troubling—and personally embarrassing—that we seemed unable to lead our way out of these crises. We poured vast amounts of money into addressing these problems, developed and introduced numerous new programs and initiatives, and even saw an increased focus from Congress. Yet, despite these efforts, we continued to struggle.

The frustration was palpable. We were leaders, trained to solve complex problems and overcome obstacles, yet these deeply rooted issues remained stubbornly persistent. It became clear that this wasn't a challenge that could be solved by resources alone; it required a fundamental shift in our approach to leadership, culture, and accountability. The weight of these challenges was a sobering reminder that as stewards of the profession, our responsibilities extend far beyond strategy and operations—we are also the guardians of the moral and ethical standards that define our Army. The battle to protect these standards was, and remains, one of the most critical fights we face.

With regard to leadership, culture, and accountability, a study by the *Harvard Business Review* titled 'How Unethical Behavior Becomes Habit' found that people with integrity issues are more likely to rationalize their conduct if it is introduced gradually rather than as an abrupt change.

The study revealed that if researchers could get individuals to cheat a little the first time, they were more willing to cheat even more the second time and eventually cheat "big" the third time.[24] In other words, they kept rationalizing and justifying their unethical actions.

I'm reminded of weapons qualification or land navigation where how you aim and pull the trigger or shoot the azimuth in the beginning is critically important over time. Being off one degree in the beginning is magnified and grows greater over time and distance until you're totally off target. Disingenuous companies and leaders often start with a "little white lie." Maybe they hedge expense accounts or tack on extra hidden fees. Over time, these actions become open secrets and part of the organizational culture.

When "little white lies" become the norm and ethical standards are confusing or unenforced, it's easy for an organization to veer away from its ethical course. I am not referring to a solitary "honest mistake" which can be addressed with counseling or remedial training but a culture where employees not only accept but feel empowered to engage in misconduct. This misconduct is easily rationalized "since everyone is doing it". In spite of everyone else, we must analyze our choices to ensure that we're doing the right thing, the right way!

Authentic Leadership author, Bill George explains this premise very succinctly when he wrote,

> *Your ethical boundaries set clear limits on what you will do when you are tempted or under pressure or when you start rationalizing marginal decisions. If you establish clear boundaries early in life, your moral compass will kick in when you reach your limits and tell you it is time to pull back, even if the personal sacrifices may be significant.*[25]

This life of integrity means we can look in the mirror without questioning ourselves. Our lives and our actions become transparent and life becomes quite simple. Remember my earlier comment about living my adult life in three roles: Soldier, Officer, and Minister. Well, rather than a life of complication, life became quite simple because there was nothing to hide or compartmentalize. As a by-product of living in the public eye, my life was an open book for everyone to see.

I didn't have to worry about the high cost of unethical actions. Costs like losing Edith's trust and respect, having my daughters, Krystle and Amber, question their dad's credibility and honor, bringing shame to my extended family, destroying my example for those who look up to me as a role model, losing my own self-respect, and negatively affecting my personal faith, which is my anchor. Once again, perfection is unattainable, but the ultimate goal is to do the right thing, even when it isn't popular or easy, because the long-term costs far outweigh the short-term pleasure.

The Core of Credibility

I mentioned the high cost of any unethical action which could cause my family to question my credibility. Credibility is that elusive quality upon which trust is built and it derives its strength from two vital pillars: character and competence. Let that sink in… character and competence. These two elements form the cornerstone of how we are perceived. They define our reliability and authenticity in both personal and professional interactions.

Character, the foundational aspect of credibility, is deeply rooted in the soil of integrity and intent. It's not merely about adhering to a set of moral principles; it's about weaving those principles into the very fabric of our being. Character calls us to align our actions with our values, forging an unbreakable link between our words and deeds. In this alignment, character becomes the bedrock of credibility.

At the core of character lies integrity, a steadfast commitment to honesty, ethical conduct, and moral rectitude. Integrity is the compass that unfailingly guides our choices, even in the face of adversity or temptation. It is about keeping promises, being truthful, and doing the right thing, not because of external pressure, but because it resonates with our innermost convictions. I carried my integrity to the witness stand, whether my testimony was required for a criminal or civil trial or an administrative personnel board hearing.

Yet, character transcends integrity alone; it encompasses the intent behind our actions. Genuine care for the well-being of others becomes the driving force of character. In this sincerity, we find a deeper understanding that our actions should not merely serve our interests but should contribute to the collective welfare. Character is not self-serving; it is the embodiment of empathy and compassion.

However, while character lays the foundation of credibility, competence constructs the edifice upon it. Competence represents the practical dimension of credibility, where skills, knowledge, and the ability to execute come into play. It's not enough to be well-intentioned; we must also possess the capacity to deliver on those intentions effectively.

Credibility thrives when competence is visible and flounders when competence falters. Therefore, competence necessitates ongoing development and refinement — a commitment to staying relevant and adaptable in a swiftly changing world. It's about honing our craft, expanding our knowledge, and refining our skills to remain capable and dependable.

> **Credibility thrives when competence is visible and flounders when competence falters.**

In the grand tapestry of credibility, character and competence are not separate threads but are intricately interwoven, reinforcing each other. Character, rooted in integrity and intent, drives the "why" of credibility, while competence defines the "how." Together, they shape the essence of our credibility, reflecting both who we are and how we are perceived by others.

The enduring power of credibility lies in its ability to foster trust, a priceless currency in human interactions. Trust is the fertile ground where collaboration, cooperation, and meaningful relationships take root and flourish. It is trust that enables people to count on our promises, have faith in our abilities, and believe in our intentions.

Nonetheless, the path to nurturing credibility is not always smooth. While competence is an area where we often feel comfortable and proficient, character can be more elusive, as it continually tests our foundations. It's the ongoing journey of aligning our actions with our values, of ensuring that our intentions remain pure, and of cultivating the genuine caring that character requires. Unfortunately, too many leaders and organizations have placed a greater value on competence while sacrificing character on the altar of success and mission accomplishment.

In essence, credibility is not a static trait but a dynamic, multifaceted attribute that requires continuous attention and nurturing. It emerges as a harmonious union of character and competence; the two pillars that not only shape credibility but also define our reliability and authenticity.

Character, firmly rooted in integrity and genuine care, serves as the moral and ethical foundation upon which credibility is built. Competence, on the other hand, provides the practical abilities and skills that lend substance to this credibility. Together, these elements form the bedrock of trust, the cornerstone of our relationships, and a defining aspect of our core values, which in turn shape our lasting impact on the world.

As we reflect on the intricate tapestry of credibility, it is essential to pause and introspect, identifying and firmly establishing our core values. These are the values we hold dear—the ones we refuse to compromise for expedience or gain.

With these core values as our foundation, we can navigate life's myriad choices and dilemmas, scrutinizing each through the unwavering lens of our principles. It is through this integrity of action that we earn the trust of our families, leaders, and teams.

Because integrity is the very foundation upon which life, legacy, and leadership are built, it holds profound importance. It serves as an anchor that grounds us in our principles and guides our decisions. In a world yearning for trustworthy leaders, integrity shines as a beacon, demanding character, courage, and conviction.

Demonstrating integrity is not merely a lofty ideal; it's a practical choice that speaks volumes about our character. It's a commitment to consistent, ethical action in every aspect of our lives. By consistently showing that our actions align with our words and values, we convey to everyone around us that we can be trusted, relied upon, and followed.

In the grand framework of life, legacy, and leadership, character stands as an enduring testament to who we are and what we represent. It fuels our journey, guides our choices, and defines our impact. When others see that our character remains steadfast, they gain confidence in our leadership and respect for our values.

In conclusion, character is the bedrock of credibility, and integrity is the cornerstone of character. Consistently demonstrating integrity earns the trust of those we lead, inspire, and influence. Character, with integrity at its core, is the mark of an excellent leader—one who leads not just by words but by the example of their actions. In a world hungry for trustworthy leaders, it is character that distinguishes the excellent from the ordinary. Demonstrate integrity and show everyone you can be trusted. Character: Excellent. **Guard Integrity.**

Reflective Questions for Chapter 3

As we close this chapter on integrity, consider how your actions align with your core values, and where there might be room for growth. Use these questions to evaluate the strength of your character and your commitment to doing what's right, even when it's difficult.

1. How do your values and experiences align with the legacy of leaders like Corporal William Roper? What lessons from their sacrifices resonate with your own life and leadership journey?

2. In what ways do you embody integrity in your leadership? Can you identify instances where you've compromised your values, and how can you learn from those experiences?

3. Reflect on a challenging ethical situation you have faced in your career. What did it reveal about your character and integrity in that moment? How did it shape your approach to leadership?

4. How can you actively foster a culture of trust within your organization? What specific actions can you take to ensure that integrity is not just a principle but a daily practice?

5. What steps will you take to ensure that you consistently develop both your character and competence as a leader? How can you seek out feedback and create an environment where others feel comfortable providing honest assessments of your leadership?

Chapter 4: Practice Discipline

"Today do what others won't so tomorrow you can accomplish what others can't."[26]

- Jerry Rice

DISCIPLINE IS A MULTI-FACETED WORD which elicits different reactions based on the experiences of the reader. For some, discipline is associated with punishment or corrective actions, such as disciplining a child. However, I see discipline from a different perspective. To me, discipline is doing what we may not want to do simply because it is the right thing to do. It is an acute awareness and an unrelenting desire to get the small things right.

My inclination to ensure accuracy frequently leads to the creation of lists. I readily admit that I am a dedicated list-maker, even in this era of electronics and technology. I find that I am most productive when I rely on the tried-and-true method of jotting down tasks on a notepad. There is something deeply satisfying about checking off completed items, as it gives me a profound sense of accomplishment. I'll even concede that I occasionally take it a step further by accomplishing a task that wasn't initially on the list, just so I can promptly add it and then cross it off. It's as if I seek recognition, even if only in my own mind!

I made my first substantial list when graduating high school. I still have my memory book at home where on the last page it asked about our life goals. As a goofy 17-year-old kid, I wrote down my life goals: becoming a police officer, serving as an Army officer, and marrying a sweet, pretty woman who understood me. I have often shared that list in elementary and high schools, speaking with students about the power of choice.

It all started with the act of writing. This transformative process allows us to transcribe the visions and aspirations of our hearts onto paper or into the digital realm, where they take on a tangible, almost *motivational* quality.

Seeing our goals and dreams in written form gives them substance and significance beyond mere abstraction. They no longer remain elusive wisps of imagination but instead become distinct, attainable objectives. It's as if, by virtue of writing them down, we've kick-started the momentum that propels us toward their realization. In fact, the Bible speaks to this momentum in the Old Testament book of Habakkuk, chapter 2:2 (NKJV) where it says, "Write the vision and make it plain on tablets, that he may run who reads it." This simple process begins with writing, followed by reading, which ultimately leads to action.

The written word carries a weight of commitment that mere thoughts lack. When we put our aspirations in writing, we declare to ourselves and the universe our intent to pursue them. It is a contract of sorts, a solemn promise to ourselves that we will strive, persist, and persevere until those dreams are transformed into reality.

Moreover, committing our goals to paper or digital form fosters clarity. It forces us to refine our ideas, strip away ambiguity, and distill our desires into precise, actionable steps. Through this process of crystallization, we gain a deeper understanding of what our dreams truly entail and the paths we must take to attain them.

The written word also serves as a powerful reminder. We can revisit our written goals and dreams whenever we need motivation, inspiration, or reassurance. They become our compass, guiding us when we lose our way, and our anchor, grounding us when the storms of doubt and uncertainty threaten to sweep us off course.

Furthermore, sharing our written goals and dreams with the right people adds a layer of accountability. When we verbalize our intentions, we invite support and encouragement from friends, family, and mentors. They become our allies, cheering us on as we strive to bring our dreams to fruition. The knowledge that others believe in our potential can be a powerful driving force.

In essence, writing down our goals and dreams serves as the keystone of personal empowerment. It ignites a transformative process that propels us from the realm of mere wishes and aspirations into the realm of purposeful action and achievement. It imbues our dreams with the energy and motivation needed to persevere through challenges and setbacks. It is, in every sense, the act of authorship that allows us to craft and rewrite the magnificent story of our lives. So, as we hold that pen or sit before the keyboard, let us recognize the immense power we wield, for we are the authors of our own destinies, and the ink of our intentions can script a future filled with purpose and fulfillment.

Five phases of a dream

I didn't understand any of this when I wrote those three goals at age 17, but I learned that personal discipline is essential to following through and building dreams through diligent action. I believe there are roughly five phases to achieving success in any dream of significance.

First, there's the **"It's beginning"** phase, which is filled with excitement as you embark on a new journey.

This euphoria is quickly followed by the **"It's difficult"** phase, where doubt and uncertainty creep in as the reality of the journey proves to be more challenging than first imagined. Unfortunately, most people surrender here. They throw their hands up in frustration and walk away because they realize it's hard and requires sacrifice.

However, if they hold on and press through, they can enter the third phase, **"It's possible."** Here, small signs of progress emerge, providing renewed motivation to keep pushing forward.

The **"It's possible"** phase then transitions into the much desired **"It's probable"** phase because momentum has become irreversible. Orders are coming in, the business is taking off, you've completed another college course, and you can see the beginning of success.

Finally, you enter the **"It's complete"** phase, where you celebrate and enjoy the fruits of your labor. Looking back, you realize that every challenge, every disappointment, and every personal sacrifice was worth it.

I wish I could say that every dream, every business, and every personal journey successfully transitions from "It's beginning" to "It's complete," but you and I both know that the highways of life are scattered with broken dreams, bankrupt businesses, and lives that have veered off track and lost their sense of purpose. I think discipline is the characteristic which is quite often missing in the tool-bag. Why is it that some people quit, while others power through? Some can "take a licking and keep on ticking"[27] as in the old Timex watch commercials while others are defunct and tossed aside. It could be the illusion that things will be easy when we know anything of value requires discipline, sacrifice and a bull-doggedness to not give in. In fact, part of the Soldier's Creed is, "I will never accept defeat, I will never quit!" So there's an admission and realization up front that this life and this mission will be hard and complex.

We must come to the realization that we don't saunter down a path of success or simply drift our way into dream fulfillment. No, we must discipline our way to that kind of success and a list simply provides a measure of prioritization and accountability. Small disciplines, done consistently over time, lead to goals being accomplished and grand dreams fulfilled.

As the Police Chief of the largest police department in the state of Alabama, it is easy to get caught up in the four stars on the uniform collar, the command authority, and the weekly television interviews. However, for me, becoming a police officer was not as simple as some might think.

My wife and I were living in a public housing community near downtown Birmingham when I started my policing career in Montgomery, Alabama. The Montgomery Police Academy was known as the toughest academy in the State and sported a 50% graduation rate. They were proud of it and determined to keep it! Since I was living in Birmingham and we were too poor to relocate, I set my clock each morning for 4:30 am so I could drive the 80 miles to the academy and arrive 30 minutes before the 7:30 formation which was full of yelling, push-ups and humiliation for most. The workdays concluded with physical training, commonly known as PT where the goal was to make us drop out of the running formation so we could be punished even more. The instructors would then assign all types of homework and send us home. While the rest of the class went to their local homes, I would then drive the 80 miles in rush hour traffic back to Birmingham where the homework and uniform preparation for the next day awaited.

I developed a disciplined system in which I studied and recited my memory work while driving back and forth. This approach gave me approximately three hours of study time each day. Even today, I can still recite the Alabama Laws of Arrest and the four paragraph Law Enforcement Code of Ethics from memory.

Unfortunately, I thought I would be fired when the cadre discovered I was living in Birmingham and not the City of Montgomery. I was quickly summoned to the Academy Director, Major Grady Arnette's office. To be frank, we all feared the man since he held our careers in his hand and often made us do extra, painful PT. I remember standing at the position of attention in front of his desk, my knees trembling, as I heard his opening question. While staring over the top of his glasses, in a very stern voice he asked, "What's this I hear about you living in Birmingham?" I barely got the words out but with a shaky voice, I responded, "Yes Sir, I do." He then said the demands are too great and there was no way I could graduate the academy and live in Birmingham. I responded with "Sir, I have to." He didn't know it but I had no Plan B. Edith and I had eloped and were married one week after the academy started. She was still in college and I had to graduate so we could start a real life together in a better environment.

At that point the entire atmosphere shifted and I saw this inquisitive and somewhat curious nature come over Major Arnette. He then said, I've checked your grades, and you have an "A" average. I don't understand how you can do that and live in Birmingham. He then asked what time do you get up in the morning? I was feeling more confident then and responded, Sir, I'm up at 4:30 and in the car at 5:30. I have three checkpoints on I-65 (Interstate 65 South). I have to be at the City of Alabaster mile marker 242 at 6:00 and the

City of Clanton mile marker 205 at 6:30. That puts me in the academy parking lot at 7:00 so I can do my final preparations before the 7:30 formation.

He seemed amazed at the details and then offered me a discounted room for $12.00 a night at the contracted hotel. I must admit I declined it since it would double my expenses (It only cost me $6.00 a day to drive my Ford Escort round trip). He closed the conversation by offering assistance if ever needed. I went through the remaining challenging weeks and graduated the academy. After initially working in the communications center I began working patrol on the west side of town on the overnight shift. The west side of town had more than its share of crime and socioeconomic challenges, making the work exciting for a rookie eager to make a difference in the lives of citizens. I felt completely at home in the alleys and neighborhoods that most people would write off. Coming from similar surroundings, I saw myself in the eyes of the people.

After a few years of patrol, I arrived home one morning and went to bed. It's strange how working night shift chronologically flips your whole world over! I was awakened by the very rare sound of the phone ringing. I groggily answered and heard that very same voice which questioned me in the academy office, Major Arnette! I quickly thought, I haven't done anything wrong, violated any rules or have I? It was a very short conversation as he said, I've been following your career and want you to transfer to the academy and be a full-time police instructor. Of course, I said Yes Sir! He simply said report up here Monday morning and I'll handle the transfer. He then closed the conversation by commenting, I want you to teach our police recruits the same discipline you have. To my surprise, the conversation years prior where I actually thought I was getting fired, resulted in a promotion and an outstanding opportunity.

Needless to say that instructor assignment and subsequent promotion to Corporal rocked the department. No one could understand how this young Officer could land such a prestigious assignment. People often say, "Character is who you are when no one is watching," but I've added an addendum: "Discipline is what you do when no one is watching."

Unfortunately, the naysayers only saw the prestigious drill sergeant "Smokey the Bear" hat and the day-shift assignment with weekends off. However, when no one was watching, there was a brief exchange between a grizzled 30-year veteran and a trainee.

That conversation motivated that leader to ignore seniority and other customs and take a chance on a kid whose disciplined habits he remembered from years before.

That successful academy assignment led me to the Hoover Police Department (HPD) when one day, Major Arnette called me into that same office and asked, "Do you ever think about going home to Birmingham?" I responded, "Yes sir, every day." He didn't know I was spending every weekend in Birmingham with Edith and she would spend her off days in Montgomery with me. HPD sent their new officers to the Montgomery Academy for basic training so there was a connection. Major Arnette recommended me for employment there and gave an extremely strong reference. In fact, when the background investigator visited the academy, those in the room quoted Major Arnette as saying they'd be fools not to hire me. The City of Hoover gave me an opportunity to return to my family in the Birmingham metro area which then decades later opened the door for my becoming the Birmingham Chief of Police.

Build into your gift

In today's get it quick, instant response society it's easy to lose focus and diffuse our attention across too many places, activities and assignments. But the engine of discipline drives us to beat the same drum over and over as we improve our gifts and talents. In other words, we must build into our gift. So what is your talent? Your purpose? Your passion? Focus on improving that gift because that gift is not just for you but also for those around you.

Let me be clear, it's not easy. It's not easy learning a new skill, a new position, or speaking a second language. Especially when it appears those around you have it easier. There were many nights on my drive back to Birmingham when I thought about the other trainees already being home, eating dinner, and doing their homework, while I was still on the road after another grueling day.

Mentally, I came to realize that comparing myself to others would never lead to victory or make the drive any shorter. At the end of the day, we are often our own biggest obstacle, and no one can hold you back like you. To counter this internal enemy, we must be self-disciplined in our thoughts, decision-making, speech, and behavior.

Could it be that the enemy is really the inner me? Just a thought...

This concept brings to mind a perspective I encountered years ago: The Gap Theory. This theory offers a unique insight that resonates deeply with the human experience. It suggests that the most significant gap in the annals of history is not a geological or temporal one, but rather the chasm that exists between our knowledge and our actions. Undoubtedly, contemporary social and health psychology research has brought attention to the discrepancy between intention and action. This discrepancy highlights the common occurrence where intentions fail to materialize into concrete behavior.[28]

> The Gap Theory is the chasm between our initial intentions and eventual actions.

In essence, scientific communities acknowledge that the mere provision of information and the development of good intentions fall short of inducing behavioral change. This idea reflects the human condition, highlighting how often we fail to translate our understanding into tangible actions. Simply put, knowing better does not necessarily mean doing better.

The Engine of Discipline

Discipline, the guiding force that bridges this gap, boils down to a straightforward principle: consistently carrying out what we recognize to be the right course of action, irrespective of the challenges that confront us. This encompasses a resolute commitment to executing tasks, adhering to values, and pursuing goals that align with our awareness of what is right or necessary. The concept of discipline comes alive when we remain steadfast in the face of obstacles and willingly endure personal sacrifices, even when faced with criticism for our choices. Discipline is a gradual process that demands time and commitment, especially in the military, where three key elements are indispensable to our fighting force: trust, discipline, and fitness.

These elements are meticulously cultivated through consistent practice, embodying the ethos of "reps and sets." Trust, discipline, and fitness evolve through repetitive actions, following the crawl, walk, run approach. We commence deliberately, ensuring every member comprehends their role, progressing gradually in challenging conditions until tasks are accomplished consistently on time and up to standard.

Discipline, as a crucial aspect of self-mastery, is a skill that anyone can develop through intentional and repeated practice. However, this proficiency comes at a cost, as every goal, dream, or vision carries its own unique price tag. The commitment to paying this price varies from person to person. Life is much like a drive-through window, you only receive what you are willing to pay for.

Jim Collins author of *Good to Great*, puts it best when saying, "Greatness is not a function of circumstance. Greatness, it turns out, is largely a matter of conscious choice, and discipline."[29]

In essence, the bridge between knowledge and action is fortified by the engine of discipline. By cultivating the capacity to align our actions with our understanding, we close the divide that has plagued humanity for generations. This union not only propels personal growth but also ignites positive change in our communities. It serves as a reminder that the true measure of our character lies not only in what we know, but in how consistently and courageously we apply that knowledge to shape the blueprint of our lives.

> **In essence, the bridge between knowledge and action is fortified by the engine of discipline.**

We're Talking about Practice

Applying that knowledge to our lives requires preparation, practice, and repetition. The National Basketball Association's (NBA) 1996 No. 1 overall pick, Allen Iverson had a 14-year NBA career which concluded as a Hall of Famer, 11-time All-Star, two-time All-Star MVP, 2000-01 MVP and 1996-97 Rookie of the Year. By any measuring stick, Iverson was a supremely gifted athlete but four days after the Boston Celtics defeated his Philadelphia 76ers in the first round of the 2002 NBA playoffs, Iverson provided one of the most remarkable and memorable rants in sports history. While talking about the value of basketball practice, he exclaimed, "We sitting in here—I'm supposed to be the franchise player, and we in here talking about practice." Iverson's frustration was evident as he went on to say, "We talking about practice. Not a game."[30] Iverson has since confessed, the "practice" rant was his way of responding to the loss of his best friend, shot and killed several months earlier, coupled with the possibility of him being traded away from Philadelphia.

Iverson's rant has been immortalized in various ways across society, appearing in shoe commercials, songs, and even a federal judge's court decision. I found the press conference and his remarks extremely interesting and insightful, and I believe they relate to the subject of discipline in five distinct ways:

1. Embracing the Grind: Practice, in sports or any other field, is often referred to as "the grind." Discipline requires embracing the grind and recognizing it as an essential part of growth and improvement. Just as athletes must practice to polish their skills, leaders and individuals must embrace the discipline of consistent effort to achieve their goals. As mentioned in Chapter 1, some people won't understand your "grind" because they don't have your dream!

2. Long-Term Perspective: Discipline is about maintaining a long-term perspective and staying focused on the bigger picture. Frustration often arises from a short-term mindset, especially when the immediate value of practice seems questionable. However, disciplined individuals recognize that practice and consistent effort are the building blocks of long-term success and growth.

3. Overcoming Resistance: Discipline helps individuals overcome both internal resistance from procrastination and external resistance from challenging circumstances. Iverson's initial resistance to practice is relatable to the common human tendency to resist tasks that require discipline, especially during uncertain and volatile times. Leaders must learn to overcome this resistance and instill discipline in themselves and their teams. In the military, we constantly encourage you to "embrace the suck." Yes, it's tough, it's grueling, and it's harsh, but it must be faced with determination and a sense of purpose.

4. Setting an Example: Discipline sets an example for others. In my opinion, Iverson's remarks on practice, while understandable in some ways, also conveyed a lack of discipline to his teammates and fans. Iverson's commitment to winning was absolutely never in doubt but leaders must exemplify discipline in their actions and their words. When leaders model discipline in both word and deed, those around them are inspired to follow suit.

5. Continuous Improvement: Discipline is at the core of continuous improvement. Whether in sports or leadership, individuals and teams must commit to ongoing learning and refinement. Iverson's later acknowledgment of the value of practice demonstrates that even those who initially resist can recognize its importance for growth and success.

In essence, Allen Iverson's famous rant highlights the initial resistance that many people have toward disciplined and consistent practice. Admittedly, his "We're talking about practice" comments have overshadowed an absolutely legendary Hall of Fame career. However, it also serves as a reminder that discipline is a crucial component of achieving excellence and long-term success in any endeavor, including leadership. Leaders must instill discipline in themselves and their teams, recognizing that it is often the less glamorous aspects of hard work and practice that lead to greatness.

At its essence, discipline is "doing the right thing the right way" which is a moral and ethical compass that guides individuals and organizations towards actions and decisions that are not only morally sound but also executed with integrity and precision. It encapsulates the profound notion that ethical behavior is not solely defined by the outcome but also by the means used to achieve it.

When individuals choose to "do the right thing," they commit to a set of principles rooted in fairness, honesty, and social responsibility. This means making choices that prioritize the welfare of others, uphold justice, and adhere to a moral code that transcends personal gain. It requires taking a stand against wrongdoing and advocating for what is just and equitable, especially in the face of adversity.

However, "doing the right thing the right way" goes beyond mere intentions; it demands a commitment to executing these principles with precision and diligence. It emphasizes the importance of adhering to ethical frameworks, following established rules and regulations, and considering the long-term consequences of actions. It acknowledges that achieving positive outcomes through unethical means is not a true victory but a hollow triumph that erodes trust and integrity.

"Doing the right thing the right way" promotes a holistic approach to ethics and morality. It reminds us that the path is not a straight line but a journey that requires continuous self-reflection, learning, and growth. It underscores the idea that ethics and integrity should permeate every aspect of our lives, from personal relationships to professional endeavors, thereby creating a foundation for a just and principled society, as well as the framework of our own lives.

After graduating high school at the age of 17. I knew a Bachelor's Degree was mandatory if I was to have any shot at reaching my goals. So that fall, I started the traditional route of college at the University of Alabama in Birmingham. I attended school and worked at night. There was no college fund, so I relied on grants, an occasional school loan and whatever income I could muster from my part time jobs and Army Reserve duty. I mainly worked in all types of restaurants but once scored the best paying job during that season of life, a full-time job loading beer trucks at the Budweiser Beer Company. Don't laugh! I didn't even drink alcohol, so it was an interesting place to work.

I went to college from 8:00 am to 3:00 pm and loaded beer trucks from 4:00 pm to about 1:00 am. We could clock out early if we finished before 1:00. Since I wasn't trained to drive the forklift to load the pallets, I used the hand truck and loaded the smaller tickets. For example, a truck might require 20 cases of one brand and 30 cases of another. While I handled those smaller fills, the forklift operator would load larger quantities, such as 80 cases of a single product.

This work schedule did not allow a lot of time for studying or socializing. I would take my books to work and study in the break room during lunch break. My only issue with that job arrangement was the nights when the veteran workers decided they wanted to leave early, so they collectively skipped lunch. Since I was the rookie, I had no voice, and definitely no vote.

I must admit, I made the Dean's List every semester I worked at the beer company. You might ask how? It was due to disciplined focus and ruthless time management. I basically had no time to waste so I didn't prioritize my schedule. No, I scheduled my priorities. You might say that's the same thing but I would respectfully disagree.

Prioritizing your schedule simply means you're ranking and assigning importance to what's on your schedule. But on the other hand, scheduling your priorities means you're ranking and

assigning value to those tasks which are important to your life: your family, your goals and your dreams. You then place those items on your calendar and now you're attending to what's important and not just the latest pop-up. I now refer to that as disciplining your calendar.

> **To discipline your calendar, don't prioritize your schedule. Instead, schedule your priorities.**

I was rocking along well until my girlfriend at the time (now my beautiful wife) called me one morning and said, I heard an ad on the radio saying the Montgomery Police Department is hiring. I was interested so we chatted a moment and knew we would see each other at school. A few days later, I heard the same ad. I called her and said, 'I'm skipping school today to drive to Montgomery and submit an application.' (Obviously, this was before online applications.)

I skipped class, drove down, applied, and was eventually hired. The minimum age to start the academy was 21. I was 20 when I applied and 21 years and three months old when I walked into the academy on my first day as a recruit.

Exciting times! However, I still had a problem since I had not finished my Bachelor's Degree. It wasn't required to be a police officer, but it was required for my life. So after graduating the academy and working patrol, I transferred to Troy University in Montgomery. The college had a great learning program for working adults with night classes and daytime options. I quickly learned that working night shift patrol and then taking an 8:00 a.m. class is not a good idea. I also learned all types of other things not related to the course work. Things like, after working all night, it's possible to sit in class and not hear a single word. It's also possible to drive home and not remember how you did it. A trip to the Registrar's Office solved that problem when I dropped the class.

I wish I could say working full time and going to school was simple and easy but I can't. It was extremely challenging with the starts and stops, moving from Montgomery to Hoover and starting over with a new police department, deploying to two wars, starting a family and all the other challenges life throws at you. By the way, this was before on-line learning simplified the distance learning process. It took a decade, but 10 years after graduating high school, I walked across the stage to receive my Bachelor's Degree.

In attendance that memorable night were my wife, daughter, my beloved grandmother, and a diverse group of well-wishers. My grandmother, a woman of profound wisdom and simple desires, had once confided in me about two things she longed to witness before the end of her journey. These two aspirations serendipitously converged on that evening in downtown Montgomery. She had expressed her fervent wish for a great-grandchild from Edith and me, and she also deeply desired to see me complete my college education. By divine timing, she cradled her six-month-old great-granddaughter in her arms while I walked across the graduation stage. It had taken a decade, a span of time that some might deem extensive, but to me, it was a journey of immeasurable worth. This pivotal accomplishment left an indelible mark on my character. It instilled in me the unyielding spirit of perseverance and resilience. Back then, my educational path had deviated from the traditional route, but it laid the foundational stones for not one but two Master's Degrees, an Honorary Doctorate, and an extensive executive leadership education at some of our nation's most esteemed institutions. It was a testament to the enduring power of determination and the boundless potential of the human spirit.

Today, I am deeply honored to serve as an adjunct professor at several esteemed universities. In this role, I find immense fulfillment in sharing my personal journey, a narrative I emphasize when engaging with my adult learners. I do this because I genuinely understand the challenges they face.

I empathize with the parent who, amid a child's battle with the flu, requests an extension for a paper submission, or the dedicated individual who, after working 20 hours of overtime last week, finds themselves with little time to participate in our discussion forums. I understand these hurdles, and I use my own experiences to inspire them to persevere, no matter how insurmountable the obstacles may seem.

I encourage them with a simple yet powerful message: even if circumstances require them to reduce their course load to just one class, they should never give up. A single class represents progress, and these small, consistent steps accumulate over time, ultimately leading to the fulfillment of their academic goals

I now challenge you to establish the daily disciplines necessary to accomplish your dreams. What obstacles are hindering your life, your legacy or your ability to lead others? What do you need to start doing? More importantly, what do you need to stop doing? Maybe you need to discipline your calendar. Maybe a "No" is warranted every now and then. Maybe you can't always be everything to everybody and still stay true to yourself and your purpose. Maybe you lack margin.

> **Calendar margin allows freedom of maneuver.**

Margin is the surplus of time allocated beyond what is strictly necessary. It serves as a safeguard for unexpected contingencies and unforeseen situations. Margin represents the space between a state of rest and the brink of exhaustion—the freedom to breathe versus the feeling of suffocation. In the military, we refer to this as "freedom of maneuver," the ability to move at will, adapt to changing conditions, and execute operations without being constrained by exhaustion, overcommitment, or lack of resources.

In essence, margin stands in stark contrast to overload. It embodies the concept of having room to spare rather than being stretched to the limit, and it starts with disciplining your calendar. Remember, there will be times when you must say "No" to good ideas in order to say "Yes" to the best ones.

Perhaps the concept of calendar discipline is new to you, and you haven't scheduled your priorities. As a result, maybe you feel like your life has gotten off track. Breaking news, we have all gotten off track at some point. In fact, some of us didn't just derail; we destroyed the track and the train!

If you could start over, what would you be? What would you do? I submit to you today that you *can* start over. It reminds me of the lyrics from a song by Christian artist Larnelle Harris:

I can begin again

With the passion of a child

My heart has caught a vision

Of a life that's still worthwhile.

I can reach out again

Far beyond what I have done

Like a dreamer who's awakened

To a life that's yet to come

For new beginnings

Are not just for the young.[31]

"New Beginnings" are not just for the young!

Did I mention that during my final two years at Troy, I made straight A's in every single class? Why? I was a little older, more focused, and definitely more disciplined.

Attending Troy was not part of my original plan. It was an unmapped stopover on my journey, and it came with its own set of challenges and dilemmas. As is the case with many crossroads, disciplined decision-making was critical, the difference between a detour and a derailment.

When I talk crisis management, I often refer to two simple questions which I believe are relevant to this discussion. For you to get the train of life back on the track and chugging towards the right destination, pause for a moment and ask yourself "What's most important Now?" The second question is "What's most important Next?" It's similar to a game of chess where you have to imagine not just your immediate move at hand but the next move thereafter. If you're not sure, take the first step but keep in mind every step we take, every decision we make has a chain reaction. You don't have to see the entire staircase in order to take the first step!

I am asking you to view discipline as a commitment to serving your future self. Your future self is your greatest advocate, deeply invested in the choices you make today. Every challenging task you conquer now contributes to a brighter tomorrow. Remember, *discipline is destiny*, the foundation upon which your future success is built.

On a more immediate level, it's about bridging the gap between future benefits and present efforts. Discipline becomes essential when an action yields discomfort initially but promises rewards later. Actions like:

- Consistently setting aside time for focused study or learning new skills

- Restricting screen time and prioritizing meaningful interactions with loved ones

- Sticking to a budget and saving a portion of income regularly

- Setting and achieving daily or weekly goals to advance personal or professional growth

- Resisting the temptation to procrastinate and instead tackling tasks promptly

I experienced this firsthand in the early days of my military career when I was woefully behind in my military education. I was commissioned as a 2nd Lieutenant at the early age of 19, but my Army Reserve unit could not seem to figure out how to get me enrolled in the Officer Basic Leadership Course. This is where I would learn the foundations of being an Army Officer. It took me four years to finally get into the course. During that time, I was leading Soldiers without any formal training beyond two years of university ROTC.

You might wonder how this applies to discipline? Well, I knew this lack of formal military education placed me behind my peers and could affect my performance and ultimately my potential. By leveraging the *Engine of Discipline*, I completed the 17-week course as an *"Honor Graduate."* I then immediately enrolled in the next course, the Officer Advanced Course, and once again earned *Honor Graduate* distinction.

As a junior captain, I completed Command and General Staff College with honors and was placed on the *Commandant's List*, a course that junior captains are no longer even eligible to attend. I earned several more academic awards, not because I was smarter than most, but because I disciplined myself and structured my calendar to be the best I could be.

It was really my competition with me. And I won!

When faced with temptation or the allure of procrastination, remind yourself of the satisfaction awaiting you afterward. By bringing future gratification into the present moment, you can redefine your habits and ultimately reshape your life's trajectory.

Don't Just Stand There, Dive In!

I remember the day like it was yesterday. Underwood Park, south side of Birmingham. I simply had no business standing in the starting block. I was about 10 years old and some kind of way, my friends and I decided we would join the community swim team, even though several of us couldn't swim. Oh, I could put my head under the water and count to 10 and maybe paddle a couple of feet but that did not qualify as swimming. But there I was, looking to my left and to my right at the other boys who looked like miniature versions of "Aquaman." This was practice and the coach was trying to decide who was best suited for each event. I can't swim so why am I here?

We knelt down, and the pistol fired; everyone quickly dived in, except me. I tried. I really did. But my body ignored my mind. I raised my arms in front of me, joined my fingers in a V-shaped pose, and told myself, "Dive, dive, dive." But I was frozen in place.

It was just as well because everyone else was swimming down the pool and did I mention, I couldn't swim. I developed a plan B. So I just stepped into the pool and stood there. I recall putting my face in the water as a starting point but for some strange reason I still didn't know how to swim. By that point, the other swimmers were returning and touching the wall as they completed their lap. They might have thought I had dived in too because I was wet, but I hadn't moved.

Isn't life like that sometimes? We have good intentions but we haven't prepared. We make emotional decisions that we haven't thought through. Our fears stare us in the face and freeze us in place. We get wet, but we were never truly committed to diving in. If I knew then what I know now, I would have saved myself a lot of grief, heckling, and embarrassment. Who knows? I might have been the first Michael Phelps if I had actually learned to swim before showing up for swim team practice. This embarrassing recollection reminds us we'll never "find" time but we must "make" time. Our good intentions must be channeled into action and a good starting point is disciplining our calendars to create the "when" and "where" because good intentions are good, but not good enough.

In 1965, a study[32] was done at Yale University. Graduating seniors were educated about the dangers of tetanus and given an opportunity to get a free inoculation at the health center. It was free and the majority of the students were convinced they needed to get the shot, yet only 3% of them followed through and got the vaccine. Why? If you don't define when and where - 3% chance of success.

There was another test group given the same lecture with one caveat. They were also given a copy of the campus map with the location to the health center circled on it so they knew where to go. They were also asked to take out their calendars and determine when they would get the shot. The results were nine times as many students in the test group got inoculated. This is not rocket science… Good intentions are good, but they're not good enough! To transform good intentions into tangible results, it's essential to translate them into actionable steps. A highly effective starting point is to structure your calendar with clear answers to the "when" and "where" of your intended actions.

Consider this powerful concept: each night, diligently record the tasks and objectives that must be accomplished the following day. When you achieve these daily goals, it's not merely a successful day; it's a building block for a brighter future. Now, picture the transformative potential of consistently chaining together seven such productive days, forming a week, a month, and ultimately, a year of remarkable progress. As John Maxwell stated, "The secret of your success is determined by your daily agenda."[33]

Undoubtedly, there will be moments when you stumble or miss the mark, no journey is without its occasional detours. However, imagine a scenario in which you consistently achieve your objectives, succeeding at least 80% of the time. How radically different would the landscape of your life appear?

This practice is akin to forging a path of purpose and discipline, where each day's accomplishments build upon the last, constructing a solid foundation for your aspirations. It is the art of transforming intentions into tangible results and gradually shaping a life that reflects your ambitions and potential.

The Cascading Power of Consistency

Consistency is the bridge between setting goals and achieving them. It's the thread that weaves intention into action transforming aspirations into tangible results. Living a life of discipline requires making a conscious choice to maintain consistent effort, day in and day out.

This consistency is the cornerstone of a disciplined life, and its importance cannot be overstated. It serves as the bridge between our intentions and actions, transforming our goals into tangible realities.

For an in-depth exploration of the benefits of consistency and how it influences discipline, refer to Appendix A: The Cascading Power of Consistency.

As great as he was, Iverson's rant that we previously discussed reflected a momentary frustration with the idea of practicing, which is often seen as repetitive and demanding. However, discipline is about committing to consistency in one's efforts, even when it may not seem glamorous or immediately rewarding. Though it's not the most exciting or enjoyable part of the journey, in both leadership and life, being disciplined means showing up and putting in the work.

Living a life of discipline requires consciously choosing to maintain consistent effort in the day-to-day, every day. It is the cumulative effect of these efforts that ultimately propels you toward your desired outcomes, making consistency an indispensable ally on your disciplined journey.

As you reflect on this powerful concept and embark on the journey of daily goal setting, visualize the masterpiece of accomplishment you are crafting, day by day, week by week, month by month, and year by year. Each step brings you closer to the life you envision: a life defined by purpose, productivity, and the fulfillment of your aspirations. This concept underscores the abundance of opportunities available in the world while emphasizing that seizing them requires a bold, adventurous, and disciplined spirit.

Instead of merely observing from the sidelines, individuals must be willing to metaphorically "dive in," to plunge into the depths of uncertainty and take calculated risks in pursuit of their goals.

Just as diving into a pool requires courage and confidence, seizing opportunities often entails embracing challenges and navigating through obstacles. It's about being willing to fully immerse yourself, despite potential discomfort and in defiance of fear.

By adopting this mindset, individuals can tap into their inner resilience, creativity, and determination. They learn to overcome setbacks, adapt to changing circumstances, and ultimately, emerge stronger and more successful.

Fundamentally, this discipline encourages individuals to embrace the exhilarating adventure of pursuing opportunities, diving headfirst into the unknown, and discovering the depths of their own potential.

So, go ahead, jump in! Or should I say, dive in? When we jump, there is always the possibility of landing on our feet. However, diving signifies an unquestionable shift in mindset, a commitment to purposeful action, and a blueprint for building a foundation for life, legacy, and leadership. **Practice Discipline.**

Reflective Questions for Chapter 4

Discipline is often the difference between merely setting goals and achieving them, so take a moment to examine your habits, mindset, and approach to challenges.

Are you practicing the discipline needed to reach your full potential? Use these questions to pinpoint where you may need to cultivate greater consistency and focus in your life.

1. When have you found yourself resisting discipline, and what was the outcome? How might things have been different if you had embraced discipline in that moment?

2. What are the small, consistent actions you can take daily to align with your goals or dreams? How can list-making or another system help you track these?

3. Think of a challenging situation where you persevered. What inner discipline did you rely on to keep going, and how did it shape the final outcome?

4. Reflect on a time when a lack of discipline led to missed opportunities or incomplete goals. What did you learn from that experience, and how can you apply that lesson now?

5. What personal gifts or talents have you neglected because of a lack of discipline? How can you start building into them today to make them stronger for the benefit of yourself and others?

Chapter 5: Cultivate Excellence

> "If you are going to achieve excellence in big things, you develop the habit in little matters. Excellence is not an exception, it is a prevailing attitude."[34]
>
> - General Colin Powell

LEADERSHIP DEMANDS A THOROUGH UNDERSTANDING of this truth: certain attributes hold paramount significance, transcending others in shaping the framework of life, legacy, and leadership.

Foremost among these virtues is undeniably excellence. The essence of the term excellence encapsulates the profound yearning to be peerless, exceptional, and to radiate brilliance amidst the ordinary. It is the relentless pursuit of continuous growth, a commitment to elevating one's own standards, and the unwavering resolve to shine brightly in a world often content with mediocrity.

However, excellence must be cultivated. To cultivate means to nurture, foster, or promote the development and growth of something, whether it be a skill, a relationship, or a particular quality. It involves deliberate efforts and actions to encourage the flourishing and improvement of an idea, a practice, or a desired outcome. To cultivate excellence means to foster an environment or mindset where the pursuit of outstanding performance, continuous improvement, and the highest standards of quality are encouraged and prioritized.

In the grand journey of existence, excellence serves as both the guiding star and the destination itself. It is the driving force that propels individuals to reach their fullest potential, igniting the fires of aspiration and compelling them to consistently surpass their previous accomplishments. A leader who embraces the principle of excellence not only strives for personal greatness but also inspires and empowers others to embark on a similar journey of self-improvement and distinction.

At its core, excellence is the foundation upon which life, legacy, and leadership are built. As leaders lead by example, setting a standard of unparalleled dedication, commitment, and performance, excellence becomes the bedrock upon which enduring legacies are forged.

By embodying the essence of excellence, leaders leave an indelible mark on their own lives and the lives they touch. They forge a path that illuminates the way for others to follow.

At its essence, excellence signifies a commitment to pushing boundaries, surpassing expectations, and consistently delivering the highest quality in all that we do. When we strive for excellence, we place ourselves on a path of continuous improvement, where good enough is never acceptable.

Being preeminent is to be at the forefront, the very best in a given field or domain. It means setting the standard by which all others are measured. Those who embody excellence not only excel in their chosen endeavors but also inspire and lead by example. They become the benchmark against which others gauge their own efforts.

The concept of standing out is a vital aspect of excellence. It's the acknowledgment that in a world filled with ordinary, excellence is the beacon that draws attention. It's about distinguishing oneself through exceptional skills, unwavering dedication, and an unrelenting pursuit of distinction.

Excellence, therefore, is not just a lofty ideal; it's a commitment to a way of life. It's the realization that mediocrity is the antithesis of progress and that to truly make a mark in any field, we must consistently aim for excellence. It encourages us to challenge ourselves, innovate, and invest the time and effort needed to be truly outstanding.

Excellence is not a destination but a journey, one marked by continuous learning, self-improvement, and unwavering dedication to becoming the best we can be. It's a path that, when chosen, not only benefits the individual but also elevates the standards of entire communities and industries.

Excellence often emerges from the little things, but it's these very subtleties that lay the foundation for grand achievements. Thus, we find ourselves entrusted with the responsibility of being diligent stewards in our present roles and responsibilities. I refrain from merely urging you to "do your best," for sometimes, your absolute best may not suffice in the current context. The crux lies in recognizing that beyond your current capabilities exists a realm where growth and improvement await. Embracing this journey entails rigorous training, invaluable mentorship, and a relentless quest for constructive feedback.

The essence of personal and professional growth lies in our ability to be diligent and excellent right where we are, at this very moment. This principle reminds us that waiting for the next promotion or a better assignment to start giving our best is a flawed perspective. In fact, such faulty thinking not only hinders our progress but also sends the wrong message to ourselves and those around us. We must remember the test of faithfulness is right where you are; not the next assignment or promotion.

Being excellent means consistently putting in our best effort, irrespective of our current position or circumstances. It means approaching our tasks with dedication, attention to detail, and a commitment to quality. By embracing excellence in our current roles, we not only demonstrate our worthiness for future promotions or assignments but also maximize our potential impact in our current capacity.

Excellence should be a continuous pursuit, not a future aspiration. Believing that we will only excel when we attain the next level implies that we're not fully engaged in our present responsibilities. It's essential to understand that promotions and new assignments are often granted to individuals who have proven their dedication and excellence in their current roles. With this attitude of diligence and excellence, we not only increase our chances of advancement but also create a reputation for reliability and competence.

> **Excellence should be a continuous pursuit, not a future aspiration.**

Furthermore, this mindset encourages a deeper understanding of the work we're currently doing. It prompts us to seek opportunities for improvement and innovation, even in seemingly mundane tasks. This perspective shift fosters personal and professional development, as it allows us to continually learn and grow in our roles.

Ultimately, excellence is a journey that begins right where we are. By embracing this mindset, we not only enhance our own prospects for success but also contribute positively to our organizations by fostering a culture of excellence and continuous improvement.

Each of us must conduct a self-check or personal inventory and ask: What do I put up with? What do I tolerate? Because what you tolerate, you will never change.

If you tolerate mediocrity, you will inevitably produce mediocrity. But it goes beyond that. People will also reflect mediocrity back to you. Simply put, you cannot offer mediocrity yet expect excellence in return. It's like planting apple seeds but expecting grapes. That's faulty thinking and misplaced expectations!

Insights from a Cup of Juice

As a senior law enforcement leader, I had the opportunity to attend the prestigious FBI National Academy at Quantico, VA which is the premier law enforcement executive leadership academy in the profession. The 11-week training curriculum attracted law enforcement leaders from all over the world. These leaders of performance and even greater potential were able to step away from the stress and strain of their demanding careers and enter this 11-week retreat of academic, physical and social renewal. Since my class was the 200th session and the first to graduate in the year 2000, the academy staff decided to forego the usual graduation at the FBI Academy in Quantico, Virginia, and instead selected Constitution Hall in Washington, D.C., as the graduation venue.

After the ceremony, my family and I joined some colleagues for a late lunch at a very noteworthy restaurant in DC. Our youngest daughter, Amber, was just shy of three years old when a very dapper-looking waiter took everyone's drink orders. Without hesitation, Amber responded, "Apple juice." We quickly informed her that this restaurant did not serve apple juice. The waiter concurred and apologized that they didn't have apple juice, so we ordered Amber a different option.

As we conversed and chatted about the academy experience, the waiter arrived carrying the tray of drinks. Imagine our surprise when we glanced at the tray and spotted a cup of apple juice! The waiter presented Amber with her cup and Amber's smile was priceless! We're still not sure how he pulled it off or who had to run down a D.C. Street to find it, but Amber was thrilled.

Can you imagine the conversation in the kitchen when our waiter said he needed a glass of apple juice? I would think the initial and fair response would have been, "We're a five-star restaurant; we don't serve apple juice." However, the waiter's actions reflected his mindset, which was clearly, "Since we are a five-star restaurant and I'm a five-star waiter, we're going to find some apple juice somewhere!"

The idea that apple juice can symbolize the very essence of excellence might seem peculiar at first. However, when we peel back the layers of this concept, a profound perspective emerges. What we see is a testament to the power of exceeding expectations and pushing beyond the limits of what is required. In today's society, the celebration doesn't revolve around the ordinary, the average, or the status quo. Instead, it is excellence that emerges as the beacon. It's the standout quality that captivates our attention and lingers in our memories.

Consider a simple cup of apple juice, an everyday item that, in the hands of an individual or organization committed to excellence, transforms into a masterpiece. It's not just about pouring a beverage; it's about crafting an experience that transcends the mundane. It's the extra care taken to ensure that the juice is not merely good but exceptional, refreshing not only the palate but the spirit as well.

Decades may pass, and we may journey across the globe, encountering countless experiences and moments. Yet, amid the whirlwind of life's adventures, it's remarkable how that one cup of apple juice remains etched in my memory. It serves as a vivid reminder of the enduring impact of excellence. It affirms that excellence, whether in a simple sip of juice or in grander endeavors, has the power to leave an indelible mark.

In a world where the ordinary often fades into the background, excellence emerges as the catalyst for recognition and remembrance. It's the quality that sets individuals and organizations apart, the hallmark of those who strive for perfection in their craft. Encountering excellence is like discovering a rare gem in a sea of stones. It commands our admiration, evokes our respect, and leaves an impression that lingers long after the moment has passed.

The lesson here is that in our pursuits, whether personal or professional, we have a choice: to settle for mediocrity or to infuse them with the spirit of excellence. It's not about seeking perfection for its own sake but rather about the dedication to continuous improvement, the willingness to go that extra mile, and the commitment to offering our best to the world.

So, as we journey through life, let us remember that even the simplest of things, like a cup of apple juice, can serve as a powerful symbol of excellence. It reminds us that excellence is not limited by scale or scope; it can be found in the smallest of details and the grandest of endeavors. It challenges us to paint our own pictures of excellence, to stand out, and to create experiences that linger in the memories of those we touch. For in the tapestry of life, it is excellence that adds the most vibrant and enduring colors, making each moment, no matter how seemingly insignificant, truly remarkable.

This example also implies that excellence is not about conforming to the common. The most natural and unfortunately most common thing to do would be for the waiter to simply bring us an order off the menu but if he had, he would not be mentioned in this book. And without a doubt, he would not have received an exceptionally generous tip, as we sought to reward him for exceeding expectations

Let me continue to paint this picture of excellence. While assigned to the Pentagon, my wife and I took a walk to the Air Force Memorial one afternoon. You might wonder why would an Army Officer visit the Air Force Memorial? Well, first, I was curious about the three stainless steel arcs or memorial spires which appear to soar toward the sky. Each arc soars to heights exceeding 200 feet, conjuring the vivid imagery of contrails left by the Air Force Thunderbirds as they gracefully execute a meticulously coordinated "bomb burst" maneuver.

Second, the Air Force are valued members of our joint force and bring lethality and capability to the fight. As we looked out toward Arlington and the Pentagon from our vantage point, we were reading the inscriptions on the memorial when one quote leapt off the marble and seared itself into my memory. The words were powerful, and their author is a legend among military leaders, especially for minority officers.

General Daniel "Chappie" James, the first African American 4 Star General in the Air Force is quoted as saying "The power of excellence is overwhelming. It's always in demand and nobody cares about its color."[35] Those words are engraved on the memorial, serving as a testament to the power of excellence.

Please allow me to strategically pause for a moment to correct the misconception that excellence equals perfection. We must understand that striving for excellence does not mean demanding perfection from ourselves or others—whether in our lives, our products, or our examples. This is not an open door for ethical misconduct or character issues, which can derail a leader both personally and professionally.

> **The strive for excellence is not a demand for perfection.**

Character counts! Legacy Leaders are held to a higher standard which means we can't truly be excellent until we are excellent in the unsupervised areas of our lives. Again, that does not mean we should impose unrealistic expectations of perfection on ourselves or others.

In his insightful monograph, *From Good to Great and the Social Sectors*, Jim Collins imparts the invaluable wisdom of "building a pocket of greatness" right within our current sphere of influence.[36] The notion encapsulated in these words serves as a gentle reminder that while we may not have the capacity to transform the entire world, we certainly have the power to effect meaningful change within our own chosen domains. Our scope may be limited, but our impact is boundless, for it is in these localized pockets of greatness that the seeds of transformation are sown.

The journey towards excellence, as Collins emphasizes, is not contingent on measuring ourselves against external benchmarks or the accomplishments of others. Instead, it is an internal quest, a continuous endeavor to become the best versions of ourselves. Whether we find ourselves in the early stages of life, navigating the challenges of adulthood, or embracing the wisdom of later years, excellence remains a timeless pursuit. It is the unyielding commitment to continuous improvement, the relentless pursuit of mastery, and the dedication to crafting a life of significance.

In our quest for excellence, we foster a culture of self-accountability, where our own standards become the barometer by which we measure progress. Through this self-driven pursuit of personal excellence, we organically extend the ripple of positive change to the world around us. Our dedication inspires others to embark on their journeys of self-improvement and collectively cultivate pockets of greatness that, in turn, illuminate the corners of our shared existence. So, let us heed Collins' wisdom and strive to build our own pockets of greatness. It is in these sanctuaries of excellence that we shape a better world, one corner at a time.

During my adolescent years, when it came to the realm of household chores, my grandmother had a wise adage she frequently imparted: "If you can't find time to do it right, how will you find time to do it over?" This seemingly simple question carried profound implications and resonated deeply with her unwavering commitment to nurturing a sense of excellence within us.

Her words were not merely about the mundane tasks at hand but transcended into the broader canvas of life itself. They served as a gentle but resolute reminder that the quality of our efforts mattered profoundly. In essence, she was conveying the importance of meticulous attention to detail, the dedication to thoroughness, and the willingness to invest time and care in everything we undertook. In her world, how you do anything is how you do everything.

Through this wisdom, my grandmother sought to instill the unwavering understanding that the pursuit of excellence was not an isolated endeavor but a way of life. It was an ethos that encompassed both the ordinary and the extraordinary, emphasizing that the diligence and commitment we displayed in our daily chores reflected our character and the standards by which we approached life's more significant challenges.

In retrospect, her teachings were more than just practical advice; they were a legacy of values. They left an indelible mark on my outlook, ingraining the notion that excellence is not an occasional choice but a habitual disposition. It is a principle that guides us to strive for the best in all we do because we recognize that the path to success, both in chores and in life, is paved with a commitment to doing things right the first time.

Do Common Things Uncommonly Well

"Do common things uncommonly well" reinforces the profound idea that greatness often emerges from the meticulous attention and care we invest in everyday, seemingly mundane tasks. It encourages us to approach the ordinary with an extraordinary mindset, understanding that excellence is not limited to grand gestures but can be found in the smallest details of our lives. This means if we're excellent in the small matters, we'll set a foundation for excellence in the greater areas of life.

"Do common things uncommonly well" is a call to infuse a sense of exceptionalism and dedication into even the most routine and ordinary tasks. It embodies the philosophy that true mastery is not confined to grand gestures or monumental achievements; rather, it's about consistently approaching everyday activities with a level of care and excellence that sets them apart.

By applying this principle, we transcend the idea that certain tasks are beneath us or unimportant. Instead, we recognize that these seemingly mundane activities form the foundation of our lives and work. This mindset shifts our perspective from "just getting things done" to creating meaningful experiences through every action we take. It means focusing on the details, taking the time to do things thoroughly, and refusing to settle for mediocrity. This approach not only elevates the quality of our output but also reflects our personal values and work ethic.

Doing common things uncommonly well is a reminder that excellence is a choice we make in every moment. It encourages us to challenge ourselves to find innovative solutions, improve efficiency, and inject creativity into even the most routine tasks. This philosophy fosters a sense of personal growth and accomplishment, and it encourages those around us to embrace a similar commitment to excellence.

The ability to excel in the ordinary sets the stage for success in the extraordinary. A consistent display of dedication and attention to detail not only reflects positively on us but also establishes a reputation for reliability and excellence. This principle reminds us that when executed with uncommon care and precision, our actions, regardless of how common they may seem, have the power to leave a lasting impact.

> **The ability to excel in the ordinary sets the stage for success in the extraordinary.**

When we commit to doing common tasks uncommonly well, several benefits emerge:

1. Attention to detail: A critical mindset that emphasizes the importance of meticulously observing and scrutinizing every aspect of our endeavors. It serves as a guiding beacon, leading us toward a heightened awareness of the finer points within our tasks and interactions. Whether we're in the kitchen crafting a meal or at our desk completing routine assignments with care, this mindset encourages us to immerse ourselves fully in the intricacies of the task at hand.

Similarly, in our social interactions, paying close attention to the nuances of conversations fosters deeper understanding and connection with others. The beauty of this approach lies in its ability to elevate the quality and precision of our work, making excellence a consistent companion in all that we do.

2. Personal Growth: A profound journey that unfolds when we ardently pursue excellence in our daily endeavors. It embodies our commitment to self-improvement, a journey that transcends the ordinary and propels us toward extraordinary heights. Through this pursuit, we not only sharpen our skills but also acquire a wealth of knowledge and broaden the horizons of our understanding. This process of refinement, often born from the crucible of dedication, has a transformative effect on our personal and professional development.

As we strive for excellence in the minutiae of everyday activities, we become architects of our own growth. Each task, no matter how small, becomes a steppingstone towards a better version of ourselves. This continuous evolution empowers us to tackle challenges with newfound confidence, broadening our abilities and horizons in the process. It's a journey that fosters adaptability, resilience, and a hunger for knowledge. These attributes are not only vital in our personal lives but also invaluable in our professional pursuits.

Ultimately, personal growth is the tapestry woven from the threads of our enduring commitment to excellence. It reflects our ceaseless desire to be our best selves and radiates far beyond our individual spheres to inspire other journeys of self-improvement. At its core, it is the foundation upon which our potential flourishes, thrusting us toward a future filled with limitless possibilities.

3. Innovation: The radiant offspring of our relentless pursuit of excellence in everyday tasks. It is the fertile ground upon which creativity takes root and blooms into groundbreaking ideas. When we wholeheartedly commit to excelling in even the most ordinary of tasks, we inevitably find ourselves propelled into the realm of creative thinking and ingenuity.

This pursuit of excellence serves as an impetus, urging us to constantly question the status quo. It prompts us to seek more efficient, more effective ways of accomplishing the routine activities that populate our lives. The sheer dedication to achieving excellence ignites a spark within us, inspiring us to explore uncharted territories, experiment with novel approaches, and seek innovative solutions to age-old problems.

As a leader, we must never settle for mediocrity; our pursuit should always be excellence. It's our responsibility to foster an environment where our team members are continuously inspired to bring out their best. When employees don't feel the freedom to explore their full potential, they gradually lose their motivation to innovate and excel. In contrast, when we cultivate an atmosphere that not only embraces risk but also permits occasional failures, we cultivate a culture of innovation within our organization.

By eliminating the notion that perfection is an absolute requirement, we liberate our employees and teammates to embark on endeavors they might have shied away from before. They are emboldened to embark on new ventures and pursue aspirations, even if there's a chance of initial failure. Legacy leaders understand that embracing risk is the only path to greatness. Therefore, we should actively encourage our team to take calculated risks and not fear the prospect of failure. In doing so, we empower them to unlock their true potential and drive innovation forward.

The consequences of this innovative spirit ripple outward, benefiting not only ourselves but also the wider world. Our commitment to excellence becomes a gift that keeps on giving. By uncovering more efficient methods or discovering novel solutions, we improve the quality of our own lives while simultaneously contributing to the betterment of the community around us. This virtuous cycle of innovation is a testament to the profound impact that the pursuit of excellence can have, turning the minute into the magnificent and sparking a cascade of positive change.

4. Inspiration: The glowing beacon that emerges when we steadfastly uphold a commitment to excellence in our everyday tasks. It is a silent force that possesses the power to ignite the aspirations of those who bear witness to our unwavering dedication. Through our actions, we become living testaments to the transformative potential of excellence, manifesting its influence on a grand scale.

Our resolute commitment to excellence is akin to a lodestar, shining as a source of inspiration that encourages personal and professional improvement in others. When we consistently set the bar high and surpass it, we send a clear message to those around us: achieving excellence is not an abstract dream, but a tangible reality within their grasp.

This ripple effect extends far beyond the boundaries of our individual lives. It permeates the very culture of the groups and organizations we are a part of. A culture of excellence takes root when the pursuit of greatness becomes the norm rather than the exception. Those inspired by our actions raise their own standards, and as a collective, we strive for loftier goals and greater achievements.

At its core, our commitment to excellence becomes a catalyst for a perpetual cycle of inspiration and improvement. It fosters an environment where individuals are not only encouraged but also empowered to reach their full potential. Thus, the legacy of excellence we leave behind is not just one of personal accomplishment but also of a positive, transformative influence that shapes the aspirations and actions of those who follow in our footsteps.

5. Sense of Fulfillment: A profound sense of fulfillment unfurls when we embrace the belief that excellence is not bound by the scale of the task at hand, but rather by the unwavering dedication we invest in it. This realization dawns as a beacon of light, illuminating the path to a deep and enduring satisfaction. When we channel our best effort into even the most seemingly mundane tasks, we forge a connection between our actions and the principles that guide us.

This bond between effort and principle sparks a fire of pride that burns brightly within us. It is a fire that is stoked by the knowledge that every ounce of dedication we pour into our work, regardless of its magnitude, has the power to make a difference. It's a reminder that every contribution we make, no matter how seemingly small, is an integral thread woven into the fabric of our collective journey.

As we strive for excellence, we construct a bridge that spans the chasm between the ordinary and the extraordinary. This bridge is not just a means to cross from one side to the other; it's a testament to the value we place on our own actions and a beacon of inspiration for others to follow. The satisfaction derived from knowing that we've given our best transforms into a reservoir of strength, empowering us to tackle challenges with confidence and to approach each task with a sense of purpose.

Ultimately, this sense of fulfillment is the realization that our contributions are not just fleeting moments but enduring echoes in the symphony of life. It's a reminder that by giving our best in every endeavor, we are crafting a legacy that transcends time and leaves an indelible mark on the world around us.

6. Building a Foundation: Is akin to laying the cornerstone of future triumphs. When we commit ourselves to executing commonplace tasks with an exceptional touch, we forge a sturdy base upon which we can construct our path to success. This unwavering commitment showcases not only our proficiency but also the discipline and dedication that underscore our actions. These qualities are akin to the bedrock upon which opportunities for greater responsibility and leadership are built.

By consistently performing common tasks uncommonly well, we stand as guideposts of reliability and competence. This reliability, in turn, becomes a magnet for opportunities. Colleagues, supervisors, and mentors notice our dedication and the consistently exceptional results we produce. This recognition paves the way for us to take on more significant roles, shouldering greater responsibilities within our professional spheres.

Moreover, this commitment to excellence is not limited to a solitary moment but becomes an enduring ethos. It molds us into leaders, inspiring those around us to emulate our dedication. As we ascend the ladder of success, our foundation remains a testament to the values that guide us. It serves as a reminder that true leadership is born from the ability to consistently excel in the everyday, thereby illuminating the path for others to follow.

In essence, the phrase "Do the common things uncommonly well" serves as a profound reminder that the quality of our approach to everyday life is just as significant as our relentless pursuit of grand ambitions. It beckons us to imbue our daily routines with a distinct brand of excellence, understanding that these seemingly mundane acts possess the transformative power to shape the trajectory of our lives. When we commit to performing the ordinary tasks of life with an uncommon degree of diligence and dedication, we set in motion a chain reaction of positive consequences.

Indeed, it is in the consistent pursuit of excellence within these everyday moments that we lay the foundation for a life characterized by purpose, achievement, and a legacy that endures through time. It's a reminder that greatness is not solely confined to the grand gestures and extraordinary feats but is, in fact, woven into the very fabric of our daily lives. By "doing the common things uncommonly well," we embark on a journey of self-improvement and personal growth that extends far beyond the realm of the ordinary into the extraordinary. And this transformation is only possible when we **Cultivate Excellence**.

Reflective Questions for Chapter 5

Excellence is not a destination—it's a journey of continuous improvement and learning. The questions that follow are crafted to help you evaluate your personal standards and how you push yourself beyond the ordinary. Think about the areas where you strive for excellence and those where you might be settling for less. Reflect on how you can raise the bar not only for yourself but also for those around you.

1. In what areas of your life or work have you settled for "good enough"? What steps can you take today to cultivate excellence in those areas?

2. How do you respond to challenges that demand more than your current best? How can you shift your mindset to embrace growth and continuous improvement rather than simply maintaining the status quo?

3. Think about a time when you observed or experienced true excellence. What impact did it have on you, and how can you apply those lessons to your own leadership or personal journey?

4. What are the "small things" in your daily routine that, if done with greater care and attention, could lead to significant improvements in your performance or results?

5. How do you encourage excellence in those around you? Are you setting an example that inspires others to go beyond mediocrity, and if not, how can you change that?

Chapter 6: Build Partnerships

> "Alone we can do so little; together we can do so much."[37]
>
> — Helen Keller

EARLIER I TALKED ABOUT MY arduous daily journey from the public housing community in Birmingham to the Montgomery Police Academy. The Academy Director provided me an opportunity to build an unspoken partnership which he activated several years later when he asked me to become an Academy Instructor. That day would have never materialized; in fact, there would have been no academy graduation, celebration, patrol assignment, or subsequent instructor assignment without my wife Edith's act of selfless service.

Let me transport you back to that pivotal day etched in my memory. It was an academy day, one of those days that seemed to push the boundaries of toughness and stress beyond the norm. Somehow, against all odds, I managed to soldier through until the very end. The instructors, on this particular day, seemed to be particularly unrelenting, subjecting us to grueling physical training sessions, commonly referred to as P.T. These sessions, combined with their decision to heap on extra homework, resulted in a day that stretched far longer than we were accustomed to. They tasked us with outlining a staggering 10 to 15 chapters from a myriad of law enforcement, police procedures, and legal books.

As the grueling day finally concluded, I dragged my exhausted and sore body to the car, ready to embark on the 80-mile journey back home. The drive was quiet, my thoughts consumed by the multitude of duties and tasks that awaited me before I could even think of crawling into bed. Once I arrived home, I distinctly remember starting to study the first chapter and diligently working through the outline. However, as I contemplated the growing list of remaining tasks, a creeping sense of mental fatigue began to engulf me. It was as if a dimmer switch was slowly being turned down, and the once bright purpose in my mind faded to a dull gray before plunging into total darkness. Suddenly, the thought of meticulously spit-shining my shoes, crisply ironing the military creases in my uniform shirt, completing the outlines, and somewhere in there managing to grab dinner and steal a few precious hours of sleep felt not just difficult, but insurmountable.

I recall turning to Edith, my wife of only a few months, and uttering those words that seemed to hang heavy in the air: "I'm quitting." Her reaction was a mix of concern and curiosity, as if she were trying to fathom the depths of my exhaustion and resolve. I began listing the seemingly insurmountable obstacles that lay ahead. Her response was simple yet profoundly impactful. She said, "I don't know how to spit-shine your shoes, but I can try. I'll iron your shirt and fix your plate, while you keep writing those outlines. Together, we can get this done."

And so, we did. Together, side by side, we toiled through the long and grueling night. While I feverishly wrote my outlines, Edith tackled the unfamiliar task of shining my shoes and meticulously ironing my uniform. With each passing hour, it became clear that this was not just a solitary struggle; it was a joint effort, a testament to the power of partnership and determination. As dawn began to break, we had conquered the mountain of tasks, and I was back in class the next morning, fatigue worn as a badge of honor.

In that moment of darkness, Edith's unwavering support and our shared determination illuminated the path forward, proving that together, we could overcome even the most daunting challenges. This story also gives us a powerful truth that we should avoid decision making when tired, exhausted or stressed. I'm not referring to trivial matters like what to eat for lunch but significant, direction changing, life altering decisions which require a clear mind and steady hand.

I often thought of that story and the importance of a support team when I was later assigned as an Academy Instructor. With a 50% graduation rate, you could identify the recruits with a sense of purpose, but also those that had a support team to rely on when times got tough (and believe me they would). Many of those with no sense of purpose would quit the academy the very first week, but even worse, we would occasionally have those who quit the very first day. I distinctly remember one kid who resigned after one hour. Are you kidding me? You might wonder how could someone quit a job with benefits like great health insurance, paid vacation and sick time, a lifetime pension, etc. in only an hour. Well, let me take you back.

The first morning of class was designed to be chaotic, as the new wide-eyed recruits were yelled at, dropped for push-ups and just trying to survive this new routine which was nothing like the movies. We would not use profanity or touch a recruit but just about everything else was fair game. The Mayor of the City would then arrive to welcome the recruits and basically encourage them to do their best. He would then invite the instructors up front and we would stand there at the position of parade rest with our feet shoulder width apart, hands clasped behind our backs, "Smoky the Bear" Hats pulled low, stern expressions, crisp uniforms, fresh haircuts, and jump boots glistening like the sun.

The mayor would then tell the recruits our job was to give them the best training in the State and to develop those fit for this honorable profession but he would admit some of them would not make it to graduation. He would then say something like, look to your left, look to your right, that person sitting next to you may not graduate. By that point everyone would have looked at someone else and tiny seeds of doubt would begin to creep in with thoughts like, "Is he talking about me?" The mayor would then drive the point home and say in fact, some of them knew in their hearts they were not cut out for this kind of work so don't waste everyone's time. Since the instructors were standing in front of the room and looking directly at the recruits we could actually see some beginning to think and reconsider if this profession was right for them. One young man set the record for the quickest resignation when as soon as the mayor finished speaking and the class took a break, he approached an instructor and resigned within one hour. I would imagine he still owns the record!

Now, keep in mind, qualifying for the academy is no easy task; in fact, it's a long arduous process which included a written aptitude test, a physical agility test, several interviews, an extensive background investigation, a polygraph (lie detector), drug screening, and both a physical examination and psychological test. So every single one of these recruits had already overcome tremendous odds just to sit in that classroom, but stress and difficulty can affect purpose and that's where a support team jumps in and fills in the gap. In my mind, it's akin to a pit crew during a NASCAR race. The driver's job is to focus on winning the race but the pit crew's job is to support that driver and ensure the car is running as smoothly as possible. So when that driver pulls into pit lane, his crew springs into action, checking, adjusting, replacing and repairing. Yes, when the checkered flag is waving, only the driver crosses the finish line but there's a team that's just as happy, just as committed, knowing they shared in the sacrifice necessary for the victory lap!

Within the realm of the academy, every task, assignment, and role play scenario concealed a valuable lesson awaiting discovery. My journey through the academy, initially as a student and later as an instructor, served as my inaugural crucible of leadership development. Little did I know that this would be but the first of many such laboratories, where I would come to understand that no individual exists in isolation, and the path to success is paved with the collaborative efforts of a well-coordinated team. Specifically, these partnerships provide:

Expanded Influence:

Effective leaders recognize that their impact goes beyond their individual efforts. By building partnerships and collaborations, they can influence a broader range of people, organizations, and initiatives. This expanded influence allows leaders to drive positive change on a larger scale.

Legacy Building:

Building partnerships is a key strategy for shaping a lasting personal legacy. It ensures that the leader's influence endures even after they have moved on from a particular role or organization. A well-established network and collaborative spirit can continue to benefit others long into the future.

Collective Impact:

Partnerships enable leaders to harness the collective power of diverse perspectives, talents, and resources. They can bring together individuals and groups with complementary skills and expertise to address complex challenges more effectively. Frequent conversations with my Deputy Chiefs revolved around our shared mission to "make it better." This commitment was so deeply ingrained in our ethos that my Deputy Chief of Investigations had those very words immortalized on a plaque adorning his office wall. I held an unshakable belief that our combined efforts had the potential to effect meaningful improvements.

Sustainability:

Sustainable leadership is about ensuring that the positive changes initiated by a leader continue beyond their tenure. Building partnerships contributes to the sustainability of leadership efforts by creating a support system that carries on the leader's vision and values.

Through these leadership laboratories, it becomes evident that building partnerships not only expands influence but also nurtures enduring impact, leaving a lasting, positive imprint on both individuals and organizations.

Insights from a Desert Place

"Hey, I don't believe we've met." Those were the words I spoke to a total stranger on a dusty road at the Kandahar Airfield in Afghanistan in January 2002. I'm not exactly sure why I said it to that specific person, at that specific time, when there were over 3,000 Service members on the FOB (Forward Operating Base). So in essence, there were many, many American Soldiers, Airmen, and coalition forces I hadn't met. But there was something about this young man, this peer, that stood out. We were both Majors and I extended my right hand, shook his hand and introduced myself. He said his name was Larry Naylor and we exchanged pleasantries for a few moments before each of us continued on our way.

My path to Afghanistan was a circuitous route. In 1990, as a young Captain I deployed to Saudi Arabia in support of Operation Desert Shield. Operation Desert Shield was a critical military operation conducted by the United States and its coalition allies to defend Saudi Arabia and other Gulf nations against the threat posed by Iraq under Saddam Hussein, which had invaded Kuwait.[38] Desert Shield saw the rapid deployment of troops, equipment, and resources to the region, effectively serving as a deterrent against further Iraqi aggression. It played a pivotal role in shaping the events that led to the liberation of Kuwait and the subsequent Gulf War.

However, while Desert Shield succeeded in its immediate mission of deterring aggression and protecting Gulf nations, my unit as a whole did not perform well. We were not employed according to doctrine and our well-respected commander experienced a family emergency which caused his early departure from theater and prevented his return. Despite this setback, individually several of us stood out. It was a joint environment and I worked for a Navy Lieutenant Commander. We had a good relationship where I felt like my work mattered and I was making a difference for the Coalition. As he began to trust me, he felt more comfortable assigning me important, significant duties. It wasn't long before I was the Officer-in-Charge (OIC) of the night shift. You might think the 12-hour night shift is when things are quiet.... No, not really because night in Saudi Arabia is day in the United States so I found myself engaging in important matters with military personnel stateside. We would do our shift handoff, where we briefed the oncoming shift, then went to our hooch to try to sleep during the day.

I was later awarded a Joint Commendation Medal for my duties. It was a "Big deal" for a Captain to receive an award signed by the Commander of our forces, Army General Herbert "Norman" Schwarzkopf Jr. My unit had a leadership vacuum which I attempted to fill, but in reality I didn't have the juice (authority) to correct most of the problems which emanated much higher than my pay grade. However, I must admit, I made several mental notes that if I ever commanded during a war, there were certain things I would do and others I would avoid. This simply means we can learn from both the good and bad leadership experiences.

After redeploying and returning home, my Army Reserve career took me to other positions and organizations and to be frank, I never really reflected on those Saudi Arabia thoughts again until 2001. On a beautiful Sunday morning, September 9th, 2001, I participated in a change of command ceremony where the Army had selected me to command the same headquarters I deployed with in 1990. Yep... I was now the Commander. Things were fine for two days but on Tuesday, September 11th the world changed when a sequence of four meticulously coordinated terrorist strikes, attributed to the Islamic extremist organization al-Qaeda, targeted the United States. These heinous attacks inflicted a devastating toll, leading to the tragic loss of 2,977 lives and injuring thousands at the World Trade Center, the Pentagon, and in Somerset County, Pennsylvania.[39] Tragically, in the aftermath, many more people succumbed to illnesses such as dust-related cancer and respiratory diseases in the months and years that followed.

The World Trade Center held a deeply special place in my heart. In 2000, while attending the FBI National Academy, I had the privilege of being hosted by the New York Police and Fire Departments, who, as part of their tradition, took us on an exclusive, behind-the-scenes public safety tour of New York City's most iconic landmarks. One of the highlights was our visit to the World Trade Center. I vividly remember standing on the roof of one of the towers and calling my wife, Edith, in sheer excitement. I told her I was looking down at the Empire State Building and that I had to bring her and the girls here one day. Little did I know that just one year later, these towers would fall, and we would witness such unimaginable devastation. I still have a photo from that day on the roof, a bittersweet reminder of a moment that now carries a profound sense of loss.

In response to this cowardice act, our country launched the War on Terror and two months later my headquarters deployed to Kuwait where we consolidated before I task organized the unit into teams for split based operations across the AO (Area of Operations). I chose to lead the unit from Kandahar since that was the former Taliban stronghold in southern Afghanistan and the most challenging location in regard to risks and life support. The Marines led by Brigadier General James Mattis (who later became Secretary of Defense) were in country when we landed. The 3rd Brigade, 101st Airborne Division would later roll in for a "relief in place" and then serve as the main effort.

After several decades of conflict and humanitarian crises, Afghanistan was a miserable, drought-stricken land of suffering.[40] Kandahar Airport was a modern miracle in its day but after the war with Russia, a civil war and now the "War on Terror," it was a dilapidated remnant of its former glory. Larry was the Executive Officer for the logistics battalion under the 3rd Brigade so their duties were to establish the supply chain and logistics support so we could fight and win our nation's war. A few days after that initial meeting, Larry and I bumped into each other again and before long he was my best friend on the base. We had the same spiritual foundation, and both were married, with daughters and no sons. This really meant we were both accustomed to being told what to do!

My wartime duties and responsibilities were extremely stressful but I had a good team and now, a good friend. I served as the spokesperson for the war in southern Afghanistan, managing a world-wide strategic public information campaign with one laptop computer and a homemade desk built from a crate. Those few moments where I could exhale were priceless as we would sit at lunch, eat an MRE (Meal Ready to Eat) and share leadership challenges. We would often discuss issues as we sought to accomplish the mission while taking care of our people. We would talk and reminisce about our families, dreams, and goals. Sometimes we would just vent. As a leader you never vent down to your team. You vent laterally to a peer or vertically to your Boss but only if you have that type of relationship.

Month after month, day after day, hour after hour, we supported each other, counseled when needed and helped each other to be successful. This relationship was forged in the crucible of war, stress, and harsh living conditions. I did not fully realize the connection and partnership until Larry was given his next assignment to report to the Department of State. This meant he was leaving Afghanistan earlier than planned. I was so happy for him but sad simultaneously. I remember the night he left and as we stood there on the tarmac, we chatted, man-hugged and he got on the plane. I'm still not sure if he saw the tears welling in my eyes as he walked away. Neither of us had any idea at the time that when I said, "Hey, I don't believe we've met" that we would become brothers for life. Even now when I'm in the National Capital Region, his home is my home and his family, my family. Combat zones are the crucible for birthing blood-brothers and sisters.

Frequently, there's a prevailing misconception that partnerships exist in a perpetual state of bliss, where the skies are always clear and not a shadow of adversity looms. Partnerships often entail resilience and the inevitable friction that arises as we work diligently to refine our approaches and solidify lines of communication and collaboration. I vividly remember a transformative moment within the Tactical Operations Center (TOC). It was on one particularly quiet morning around 2:30 am when an Army senior leader made an unanticipated entrance. This General Officer's presence was nothing short of legendary in our Army. Commanding one of the Army's most esteemed divisions, he had journeyed to our location to check the welfare of his Soldiers and assess the effectiveness of our operations.

At a certain juncture, I heard his commanding voice resonate throughout the room, summoning everyone to gather closely. As we encircled him, the words he imparted that day remain etched in my memory. His initial remarks addressed the abundance of smiles within the TOC which left me somewhat perplexed, given our cohesive and proficient team. He proceeded to elucidate that our excessive happiness was a cause for concern. I recall him saying, "There's too much smiling in here." In his view, this mission held such gravity that there should be moments devoid of smiles, moments characterized by friction. This friction, he explained, would arise from the urgency of needing critical information or a vital piece of intelligence but delays are stemming from other teams or individuals. He emphasized that this conflict and friction were inherent to our dynamic environment, a battlefield in constant motion, where operations evolved in our relentless pursuit of enemies threatening the United States.

It's been quite a while but his insight and wisdom has stuck with me. He was not authorizing rudeness or unprofessionalism but every support team and every partnership will have those times of friction, disagreement and conflict. In a partnership, everyone is working and striving for the common good which brings togetherness and unity of effort but can also open wounds if you're not prepared and properly focused. Too many partnerships waiver and even dissolve when the going gets tough. Too many teams split into factions due to tribalism, lack of trust, misunderstandings and role confusion. However, the converse is also true, many people believe that they alone can accomplish their goals without any assistance. They fail to realize that any "significant" change requires assistance from others. For example, something as simple as losing weight might require a diet plan, an exercise plan, a gym membership, a personal trainer, and more. That team concept becomes even more critical as the objective grows more significant or complex.

When the stakes are high, partnerships are not just helpful—they are the foundation of success. A powerful example of this came during the high-altitude balloon incident in February 2023. When a People's Republic of China surveillance balloon entered U.S. airspace, it triggered an urgent national security response. This situation required seamless coordination across multiple agencies, including the military branches, the White House, the Department of State, the Joint Staff, NASA, the National Weather Service, and other national security organizations. No single entity could address this challenge alone; it required a network of teams working together with precision and urgency.

This wasn't just a test of our defense systems, it was a test of leadership under pressure. Every decision carried strategic implications, from protecting sensitive sites to managing international tensions. We had to balance immediate security concerns with broader geopolitical consequences while ensuring a coordinated and effective response. Because of strong interagency cooperation, we successfully executed the mission, neutralizing the balloon and bringing it down over the Atlantic Ocean near Myrtle Beach. The fact that the remnants landed in water allowed us to recover and analyze them for critical intelligence.

In moments of crisis, leaders must be decisive, clear, and composed. The clarity of purpose is what guides teams through complex situations. But just as important, this event reinforced a key truth about partnerships:

> **Complex problems require a network of teams, and team building must occur before the crisis begins.**

High-level operations do not succeed by accident. They succeed because of the relationships, trust, and collaborative frameworks built before the crisis ever emerges. The ability to unite individuals with diverse expertise, align their efforts, and work toward a common goal is what defines effective leadership. When partnerships are strong, the mission succeeds, even in the most unpredictable circumstances.

Partnerships but Politics

Regrettably, politics has the potential to infiltrate any form of interaction, be it formal or informal, involving groups of people. I witnessed it at the highest levels of the Department of Defense but even more so in law enforcement. Upon reflection, my experience in law enforcement was genuinely rewarding, fostering community relationships was fulfilling, yet the intrusion of politics proved to be undeniably frustrating. Two distinct accounts underscore this reality. Firstly, the imposition of unrealistic crime reduction targets, often set during election years, lacked a basis in pragmatic experiences or those of similar jurisdictions. Instead, these targets were solely focused on winning votes, with politicians relying on the public's swift forgetfulness post-election.

The second issue that starkly confronted me was the pervasive animosity between government branches. While tension can be constructive when channeled appropriately, animosity becomes a hindrance to progress, directly impacting the people. A vivid memory from December 2015 comes to mind: hosting national experts for a session on crime reduction in Birmingham, I received a call informing me of a physical altercation between the Mayor and a City Councilor at City Hall during an ongoing Council meeting. The embarrassment was palpable as I excused myself from a meeting on crime prevention to respond to a crime in City Hall! The incident, eventually making national headlines, diverted significant energy and effort away from more pressing matters. Dueling branches of government and political camps, public statements and accusations ultimately resulted in the city being the ultimate loser.

I see the political issues as "outliers" but overcoming politics and agendas in group dynamics requires a focus on fostering a collaborative and transparent environment. Here are some strategies that, unfortunately, were not put to good use:

1. Communication: Encourage open and honest communication within the group. Clearly articulate goals, expectations, and decisions to avoid misunderstandings.

2. Shared Vision: Establish a shared vision and common goals for the group. When everyone understands the overarching purpose, it can unite individuals despite political differences.

3. Inclusive Decision-Making: Involve all members in decision-making processes. When people feel their input is valued, they are more likely to contribute positively to the group.

4. Conflict Resolution: Address conflicts promptly and constructively. Implement conflict resolution strategies that focus on finding common ground rather than perpetuating political divides.

5. Focus on Objectivity: Emphasize data and objective criteria in decision-making. This minimizes the influence of personal biases and political agendas.

6. Leadership: Strong leadership is crucial. Leaders should actively manage group dynamics, promote a positive culture, and discourage behaviors that contribute to political maneuvering.

7. Team Building: Engage in team-building activities to strengthen relationships within the group. Building trust can mitigate the impact of politics.

8. Clear Roles and Responsibilities: Clearly define roles and responsibilities to avoid power struggles. When everyone knows their contribution, it reduces the likelihood of political maneuvering.

We must remember, overcoming politics is an ongoing process that requires commitment from all group members and consistent efforts to maintain a healthy and collaborative dynamic. Unfortunately, at that time, the leadership of the City was not focused and united in its efforts.

Despite the outliers, I encountered countless lessons in leadership and teamwork. One of the most memorable and impactful lessons came from an unexpected source — one of my dedicated Sergeants in the Homicide Division. This Sergeant had a unique habit of including a thought-provoking old African Proverb in the tagline at the bottom of his emails. It read, "If you want to go fast, go alone. If you want to go far, go together." These words, seemingly simple, held profound wisdom that has since resonated deeply within me and countless others.

The essence of this quote is clear: it underscores the extraordinary power of collaboration and the intrinsic value of working together as a cohesive team. In the fast-paced world of law enforcement, where every decision can have far-reaching consequences, this message carried immense relevance. It reminded us that while individual efforts might yield swift results, the true measure of success lay in our ability to unite, harmonize our strengths, and tackle challenges as a collective force.

The sentiment expressed in that tagline transcends the realm of policing and resonates universally. It speaks to the heart of human achievement, emphasizing that the journey toward any meaningful goal is often a marathon rather than a sprint. And to navigate this journey successfully, one needs not just a team but, perhaps, a larger and more diversified one. In essence, it's a reminder that we all require a support network, a community of individuals who stand by us unwaveringly, shoulder to shoulder, in our pursuit of success.

I found the importance of strategic partnerships profoundly evident during my tenure as the Deputy Commander of U.S. Northern Command, where I was entrusted with the monumental responsibility of defending both the United States and Canada. This task was not only vast in scope but also carried immense weight, especially when considering that much of the critical infrastructure essential for our nation's force projection lies outside the direct control of the Department of Defense. This infrastructure is vulnerable to a range of cross-domain threats, from cyber-attacks to physical sabotage, making its protection a complex and urgent priority.

Recognizing the gravity of this challenge, I regularly convened with the Deputies of the Cybersecurity and Infrastructure Security Agency (CISA) and the Federal Emergency Management

Agency (FEMA). Together, we navigated the intricate landscape of national security, working tirelessly to strengthen our collective resilience. These monthly meetings were more than just discussions; they were strategic sessions where we aligned our efforts, shared intelligence, and developed comprehensive plans to safeguard our nation's infrastructure against evolving threats, both cyber and kinetic attacks. The collaboration between military and civilian agencies was not just beneficial; it was essential for ensuring the security and stability of our homeland in an increasingly interconnected and perilous world.

So, I pose this question to you: Who forms the bedrock of your support team? Whom do you partner with in your personal and professional endeavors? Who shares your unflagging dedication to the pursuit of success, whatever that may mean to you? These are the individuals you should consider your pit crew, working tirelessly to ensure your journey is not only fruitful but also filled with camaraderie and shared purpose.

I can attest to the fact that no one achieves greatness alone. From my days of undercover narcotics operations, where it's just you and your partner enduring the monotony of stakeouts, to the pivotal moments of commanding thousands of dedicated Soldiers, a profound lesson has emerged time and again: there are occasions when we must be willing to set aside our immediate personal ambitions in favor of the enduring prosperity of the collective.

It's the collaboration, the unity of purpose, and the strength derived from a network of supportive individuals that truly propel us forward. The lesson I learned from that simple email tagline has stayed with me as a testament to the enduring importance of teamwork. It serves as a reminder that while we may embark on individual quests, our greatest successes are achieved when we embark on them together, supporting one another every step of the way.

This essence of partnership is a driving force that propels teams to extraordinary heights. It's the synergy that arises when diverse talents unite under a common banner, each member contributing their unique strengths to achieve a singular, overarching objective. It's the realization that by setting aside personal concerns and embracing the larger vision, we become architects of our team's enduring success and, ultimately, architects of a legacy that transcends our individual contributions.

I must admit this requires a mindset that refrains from defensiveness or, worse, offensive behavior when our focus converges on the unity of effort and purpose. The ability to harmonize our individual objectives with the greater mission is at the heart of true partnership. It necessitates a profound commitment to the shared goal, an acknowledgment that our collective pursuit is greater than the sum of our individual aspirations.

Building these partnerships is vital for leading a successful life, establishing a lasting legacy, and effectively leading others. These partnerships allow individuals to harness collective strengths, benefit from diverse perspectives, and offer mutual support during both triumphs and trials.

Collaborative achievements through partnerships can contribute to a legacy that endures beyond one's lifetime, leaving a meaningful mark on the world. Moreover, these collaborations cultivate leadership skills by demonstrating the ability to collaborate, delegate, and inspire others. These partnerships facilitate the exchange of knowledge and expand professional networks, opening doors to new opportunities and resources. They also enhance resilience, providing emotional and practical support during challenging times. In essence, building partnerships serve as the cornerstone for achieving personal and collective success, leaving a lasting legacy, and effectively leading and inspiring others. Make it better. **Build Partnerships.**

Reflective Questions for Chapter 6

Strong partnerships are built on trust, shared values, and mutual respect. As you reflect on the themes of this chapter, consider your current relationships and collaborations. The following questions are meant to help you assess the quality and effectiveness of your partnerships. Are you building bridges that create lasting impact? Use these questions to explore how you can nurture meaningful connections that amplify your influence and success.

1. Reflect on a time when someone supported you during a challenging period. How did their partnership influence the outcome, and what did you learn from that experience about the power of collaboration?

2. What personal or professional partnerships have been most impactful in your life? How did those partnerships shape your success or help you overcome obstacles?

3. How do you contribute to the success of others in your partnerships? What more could you do to ensure that your partnerships are built on mutual support and shared goals?

4. Think about a time when a lack of collaboration or teamwork hindered your progress. What could have been done differently, and how can you apply that lesson to future partnerships?

5. What steps are you taking to build or strengthen partnerships in your life and career? How can you foster an environment where collaboration is a priority for you and those around you?

Chapter 7: Embrace Change

> "Our dilemma is that we hate change and love it at the same time; what we really want is for things to remain the same but get better."[41]
>
> - *Sydney J. Harris*

I VIVIDLY REMEMBER THAT SPECIAL day when my Army unit and I finally returned home from our deployment in Afghanistan. Stepping off the bus at the Army Reserve Center, we were greeted by the flashing lights of media cameras capturing this momentous occasion. Amidst the joyful chaos, the air was filled with the ecstatic cries of family members eagerly searching for their beloved Soldiers.

As I scanned the bustling crowd, my heart skipped a beat when I spotted Edith's beaming smile. Our eyes locked, and an indescribable warmth washed over me. Time seemed to stand still for that fleeting moment. Then, at the appointed time, both groups—Soldiers and their eagerly awaiting loved ones—charged towards each other with a fervor that could only be matched by the intensity of their long-awaited reunion.

In that heartwarming embrace, spouses, significant others, extended family, and friends melded into one jubilant, tightly knit community. Bear hugs, passionate kisses, and tearful reunions became the order of the day, a testament to the profound bonds that had endured the trials of separation. It was a scene of pure, unbridled joy, a poignant reminder of the deep connections that make the sacrifices of military service not just bearable but also deeply meaningful.

The word embrace is often defined as to take or receive gladly or eagerly; accept willingly.[42] This means there's an excitement and welcoming when we embrace. It's easy to embrace at a Welcome Home Ceremony, or family reunion, but that's not the normal or average reaction when change is involved. In fact, there's dread, fear, and uncertainty when change occurs in our personal world. It doesn't matter whether it's personal or organizational there's a universal fear of change when it affects us. Quite often there's concern even if it's positive change. We don't embrace change, instead we run, avoid, and even hide while failing to acknowledge change is necessary and should be welcomed.

Legacy leaders possess a profound understanding that change is an enduring facet of life itself. Rather than hoping for its disappearance, they recognize that, if anything, the pace of change is accelerating in our modern, media-saturated, and technologically advanced society. In this whirlwind of transformation, change whirls faster than ever before, often bringing with it a palpable fear of loss, bewildering confusion, and the imperative to recalibrate our bearings in pursuit of the new norm.

Change, by definition, entails modification and the act of making things different. Paradoxically, many individuals find themselves dissatisfied with the status quo yet resistant to change.

It's a curious dichotomy: a desire for something better juxtaposed with a reluctance to embrace the necessary transformation. It's an age-old conundrum, akin to the adage that the only person who truly relishes change is a wet baby – a humorous yet poignant metaphor for our innate resistance to disruption.

Yet, legacy leaders not only acknowledge the inevitability of change but also embrace it as an opportunity for growth and progress. They recognize that change, when navigated thoughtfully and effectively, can lead to innovation, improvement, and the realization of new possibilities. It is this enlightened perspective on change that sets them apart, allowing them to guide their teams and organizations through the turbulent waters of transformation, ultimately leaving a legacy of adaptability and resilience in their wake.

Ralph Waldo Emerson once profoundly stated, "The only person you are destined to become is the person you decide to be."[43] This insightful quote underscores the notion that change is often a deliberate choice, stemming from a conscious decision to shape one's destiny. However, the reality of change is multifaceted, as it frequently takes on a more complex character, characterized by its imposition upon us. There are times when change is imperative even before we have a comprehensive understanding of its intricacies and ultimate outcome. It's in these very situations that the fabric of trust can fray, as those impacted by change often instinctively gravitate towards self-protection and self-preservation.

Pause for a moment and engage in introspection about the tapestry of your life. Take stock of the highs and lows. Do a quick inventory of the good, the bad and the ugly. What would you like to change right now? Make a list if necessary or scribble in the margins. What if I pointed my finger at your list and declared you are one decision away from changing that. Would you be inclined to place your trust in such a notion? Could you muster the belief required to embrace this potential for change? It's conceivable that you've grown accustomed to the status quo, perhaps even found a measure of comfort within it.

However, I urge you to consider this: what you choose to endure, what you permit to linger, is what will persist. In essence, that which you accept becomes an enduring part of your narrative. This is at the heart of why, for many individuals, change often necessitates a forceful imposition, met with resistance and reluctance. It's a testament to our inclination to find solace in familiarity, to remain where we are, unchallenged by the prospect of transformation. Your desire to change must be greater than your desire to remain the same. Quite often we see a need but there's no desire (or willingness).

In truth, we frequently remain in our comfort zones, unmoved by the need for change unless we perceive a glaring problem demanding resolution. It is within this delicate interplay of comfort and discomfort that the seeds of change must be sown. It's a reality that underscores the paradox of change—often a necessity we are reluctant to embrace because the status quo feels familiar and safe. Yet, therein lies the challenge and the opportunity for growth, as recognizing the need for change is the first step towards crafting a brighter, more fulfilling future and meaningful transformation. In 2020, the incoming 22nd Chief of Staff of the Air Force, General C.Q. Brown released his strategic approach, "Accelerate Change or Lose."[44] He knew the status quo, legacy processes and methods of operation were woefully insufficient in response to the evolving security challenges in a complex strategic environment.

In 2023, General Brown assumed the role of Chairman of the Joint Chiefs of Staff. During the meetings I attended with him, I found him to be thoughtful, personable, and strategic, with the sharp focus typical of a fighter pilot. Abruptly, in early 2025, he was unceremoniously removed from his position by the incoming Presidential administration. This unexpected change highlights a broader truth: in a constantly evolving world, change is not just inevitable, but essential. Whether it's navigating abrupt transitions or embracing ongoing transformation, we must adapt to remain relevant.

Conceptually, I believe there are three general types of change: Revolutionary, Evolutionary, and Visionary. Over the course of my careers, I've been a part of all three types of change, either as the change agent or the change recipient. Specifically:

Revolutionary Change is quick, chaotic, unpredictable and often the result of external forces. In fact, it usually results from a crisis.

Evolutionary Change is planned, programmed, and implemented gradually over time. This gradual change allows time and space for evaluation and course correction.

Visionary Change is conscious leader-initiated changes to the vision, strategy, organizational philosophy or operations of an organization. This change can be the result of external pressures, internal reflection and evaluation or the need for organizational alignment.

Before I dig too deep into change management, I must address the issue of criticism up front. Regardless of the level of change, it often brings a host of critics, snipers and opposition. However, when faced with criticism, it is crucial to assess its source and intent to gauge its value and relevance. Reflect on these "Three C" questions to effectively manage and leverage criticism for personal and professional growth:

1. Is the feedback "credible?"

Evaluate the substance of the criticism. Is it based on accurate observations and constructive advice, or does it stem from personal biases and unsupported claims? Credible feedback is grounded in reality and aimed at fostering improvement.

2. Is this person's intentions "constructive?"

Assess the motives behind the feedback. Are they aiming to help you improve, or is there a chance their intentions might be less supportive? Understanding their motives can help you determine whether the criticism is meant to assist you or undermine you.

3. Is this person "connected" to the issue?

Consider the critic's connection to the matter at hand. Are they directly impacted by your actions or decisions, or are they simply providing an external perspective? Those directly involved often provide more relevant and insightful feedback.

By carefully reflecting on these questions, you can more effectively distinguish which criticisms to accept and which to disregard, ultimately improving your capacity to learn and grow from constructive feedback.

Policing under the Shadow

My hometown didn't see a problem when Dr. Martin Luther King declared, "Birmingham is probably the most thoroughly segregated city in the United States."[45] In the year 1960, Birmingham, with a population of 350,000, was sharply divided, with 60% of its residents being white and 40% being Black.[46] During this period, the city was marred by widespread violence and the constant threat of violent acts. From 1945 to 1962, Birmingham witnessed 50 racially motivated bombings of African American homes, businesses, and churches. Even Jewish synagogues were not spared from these attacks. Shockingly, the local law enforcement authorities made no concerted efforts to apprehend those responsible for these acts of terror, and as a result, the city gained a chilling new moniker — "Bombingham."[47]

Tragically, the climate of racial tension in Birmingham was further exemplified by incidents such as the assault on renowned singer Nat King Cole in 1956. Cole was brutally attacked and beaten while performing on the stage of the Municipal Auditorium by members of the White Citizens Council. A year later, the city was shaken to its core when Klansmen abducted an innocent Black man from the streets, subjecting him to a horrifying and fatal ordeal that included castration and murder. These brutal acts, along with countless other instances of beatings, rapes, vandalism, and various forms of abuse, collectively enforced the tenets of white supremacy in Birmingham during this deeply troubled period in its history.

On a Sunday morning in September 1963, a bomb is detonated at the 16th Street Baptist Church which murdered 4 little girls attending church. That church is 5 city blocks from my former office. On that same day, Virgil Ware, a kid riding his bike was shot and killed. And thru it all, the police department was not part of the solution but part of the problem. Law enforcement is the most visible arm of government but tragically during the Jim Crow era, racial segregation of public and commercial facilities throughout the south and especially in Birmingham was legally required, absolute, and ruthlessly enforced.

The Birmingham Police Department (BPD) was the arms and legs of a racist government and the brain was the Commissioner of Public Safety, Eugene "Bull" Connor in charge of the police and fire departments. He was a virulent racist with connections to the Ku Klux Klan, and his police — some of whom were Klansmen themselves — brutally enforced the racial status-quo. He had so many kids arrested during the children marches that the BPD had to use cattle stalls at Fair Park. Our citizens remember it. I kept a small file box in my office from the 1960's which was filled with index cards. The cards were a remnant of the department's intelligence files where they conducted surveillance of the civil rights leaders and their work in Birmingham. That box served as a constant reminder of the criticality of our work to chart a new path in Birmingham law enforcement.

During that fateful summer, my father and his friends were deeply involved in the marches and demonstrations. Amid the intense fervor of those protests, a remarkable incident unfolded. At the height of the chaos, my father made a daring decision. He left his car behind in the heart of downtown Birmingham and, along with his companions, made a swift escape to our home in the Kingston area.

When I questioned him about this perplexing choice, my father's explanation shed light on the urgency of the moment. They recognized the need to vacate the downtown area urgently, realizing that there was simply no time to return to the parked car. Fearful of police arrests and brutal beatings that had become all too common during those tumultuous times, they opted for a desperate dash on foot.

In the dead of night, my grandfather stepped in as a beacon of support. Around 1:00 a.m., he bravely drove them back into town. Their mission was clear: to retrieve my father's abandoned car and, above all else, to evade the watchful eyes of law enforcement.

This narrative unveils a poignant chapter in the history of civil rights activism, where personal sacrifice and determination intertwined with the relentless pursuit of justice. It serves as a testament to the unwavering commitment of individuals like my father and the countless others who, in the face of adversity, dared to stand up for their beliefs and the principles they held dear.

I still say in Birmingham, we police under the shadow of the civil rights struggle. Those African American citizens and civil rights leaders were more courageous than the organization I was leading. Those citizens stood for right but the BPD stood for wrong. And with the civil rights era intelligence cards in my office, I was well aware of how the Police Department tracked the civil rights leaders and did everything it could to stop the movement; but courage and peaceful protests triumphed over evil.

History has a way of coloring the present. The Police Department was so brutal and heartless that the images still remain with our older generation, especially if there was an allegation of excessive force. I must also add that many of our younger officers didn't quite understand the scrutiny and why there were questions with any use of force case. In response, we implemented an initiative where we brought every new police officer to the Civil Rights Institute so they could learn the history of the city and their police department. We required them to do community projects while they were in the academy so they could learn street level community service. Fortunately, I had an amazing academy staff to pull it all together.

It's often said there are three types of people in the world; those that make things happen, those that watch things happen and those that wondered what happened. I didn't want to lead an organization that wondered what happened but our goal was to be at the forefront of this paradigm change. Hence, I was extremely proud when Birmingham was announced as one of six national pilot sites for the National Initiative for Building Community Trust and Justice which was designed to improve relationships and increase trust between communities and the criminal justice system. It was also designed to develop and implement interventions for our most marginalized victims, conduct research and evaluations; and establish a national clearinghouse. The clearing house information, research, and technical assistance would be readily accessible for law enforcement, criminal justice and community leaders. The initiative was guided by a board of advisors which included national leaders from law enforcement, academia and faith-based groups, as well as community stakeholders and civil rights advocates.[48]

Addressing culture change in police work is a complex and pressing issue that demands our immediate attention. The conventional approaches ingrained in law enforcement for decades must undergo a fundamental transformation. In low-income communities, the intersection of economic challenges and social disparities often contributes to elevated levels of crime and disorder. The intricate web of poverty, limited access to quality education, and insufficient employment opportunities can create an environment where criminal activities become more prevalent. These communities frequently grapple with systemic issues, such as inadequate infrastructure, limited healthcare access, and a dearth of social services. Consequently, residents may face heightened stressors and fewer resources to address them, potentially leading to increased crime rates. Tackling crime and disorder in these areas necessitates comprehensive strategies that address the root causes, offering support, education, and economic opportunities to foster a safer and more prosperous community.

In the current landscape, law enforcement finds itself under an unrelenting microscope, representing the most visible facet of local government. Consequently, the imperative for reform has never been more compelling, as we seek to rebuild trust, enhance community relations, and forge a path toward a more just and equitable future in law enforcement.

The National Initiative combined existing and newly developed interventions informed by those ideas in six pilot sites around the country. In collaboration with the Department of Justice, the National Network for Safe Communities at John Jay College of Criminal Justice, the Justice Collaboratory at Yale Law School, the Urban Institute and others, our goal was to design a new playbook for policing in America. With the ultimate goal being safer communities, I was willing to implement major changes to structure, policies, and culture. Regardless of the type of change, people will respond from their foxhole, and what you see is based on where you sit. I saw a community willing to partner with the department but unfortunately, some saw threats to the status quo.

Regardless of the setting or environment, I was quickly reminded there are four basic responses to change (similar to a pyramid):

1. Embrace:

At the top of the pyramid and most ideal level, embracing change is about willingly accepting and wholeheartedly welcoming it into our lives or organizations. It signifies a proactive approach, where individuals or teams recognize the value of the change and are excited to be a part of it. They employ it, and actively seek ways to create and champion the change, understanding that it can lead to growth, innovation, and progress.

2. Comply:

Compliance represents a more passive response to change. In this stage, individuals or organizations do the bare minimum required to avoid being labeled as non-compliant. They may not actively resist the change, but they also don't fully engage with it. Instead, they follow the new rules or procedures just enough to stay within the boundaries of what's expected.

3. Tolerate:

Tolerating change implies a degree of detachment or disengagement. Individuals or groups in this stage are often quiet observers, not actively participating in the change process. They may attend meetings or go through the motions, but their hearts and minds are not fully invested. They essentially endure the change, hoping it will pass without significant disruption.

4. Resist:

At the bottom of the pyramid and most resistant level, individuals or organizations openly defy and actively oppose the change. They may voice strong objections, organize resistance efforts, or sabotage implementation. Resistance can manifest in various forms, from vocal protests to deliberate attempts to undermine the change initiative.

Understanding these four levels of response to change can help individuals and organizations navigate the complexities of change management. Ideally, the goal is to move from resistance or tolerance toward embracing and employing change as a positive force for growth and improvement.

It's a beautiful aspiration to envision a world where everyone operates at their best, akin to Level 1. However, genuine success lies in elevating most individuals to Level 2 (Compliance), with only a handful remaining at Levels 3 and 4. Throughout my journey, which has allowed me the privilege of leading organizations of diverse types and sizes, my leadership in effecting change has been a mixed bag.

With the passage of time, I honed my skills, gradually evolving into a more adept change agent. Yet, leading the National Initiative proved to be one of the most formidable leadership challenges

I have ever encountered. It was a transformative process marked by the intricate interplay of politics and the presence of adversaries both within and beyond the department's confines. Being totally transparent, I found there were several stakeholders and observers, some within the department and others in the community, who benefitted from the status quo and had no desire to see improved police-community relations. In fact, there were many attempts to sabotage our efforts since they were a threat to their way of life and/or pocketbook! In fact, I recall a meeting in my conference room where one notable community activist asked for payment for his partnership and support. Needless to say, that didn't happen but it tainted the relationship, and I was determined to work around him.

My challenge involved navigating the introduction of a data-led, intelligence-informed policing approach while addressing the complexities of community disorder and fairness in low-income areas. Striking a balance was a nuanced undertaking. Although a zero-tolerance approach can yield immediate crime reduction, as observed in Birmingham, it demands a nuanced implementation, considering the socio-economic factors influencing low-income neighborhoods. Overly aggressive enforcement may erode trust between law enforcement and the community, impeding cooperation and escalating tensions. Hence, strict law enforcement needs to be complemented by community-oriented policing strategies that delve into the root causes of crime, engage residents, and foster collaboration.

Fortuitously, we collaborated with National Network Director David Kennedy and colleagues to implement the Group Violence Intervention (GVI) Initiative. Originating as "Operation Ceasefire" in Boston during the 1990s, GVI aims to reduce street group-involved homicide and gun violence. This initiative, founded on data from the National Network for Safe Communities, targets the 0.05% of the population consistently associated with 75% of violent crime. The strategy focuses sharply on small groups most likely to engage in or be victims of violence in the near future. Additionally, the City of Birmingham was designated as one of the Department of Justice's Public Safety Partnership (PSP) Cities. PSP offered an innovative framework for collaborations across local, state, and federal levels in investigating, prosecuting, and deterring violent crime, particularly related to gun violence and gangs.

I remain so grateful for the host of partners and supporters who stood beside us; federal, state, local, faith, community, private and non-profit. My mindset was the only thing better than a team was a bigger team!

I must also underscore the importance of trust which is the foundation upon which successful culture change is built. Trust creates an environment where people feel safe, empowered, and motivated to embrace new cultural norms and work collectively toward the desired cultural shift. Without trust, resistance, skepticism, and even sabotage can hinder culture change efforts, making it difficult to achieve the intended transformation.

One might assume that in highly regimented, militarily structured organizations, initiating change would be a straightforward endeavor—simply issue an order, and individuals will commence their march toward the new directive. However, the reality of change management proved to be far more complex, consistently presenting similar challenges, regardless of the mission or the organization at hand. The process of effecting change often resembled navigating a treacherous terrain, marked by resistance, skepticism, and the need for skillful navigation to steer the ship of transformation towards calmer waters.

I often find myself reflecting on the remarkable police officers who stood alongside me throughout those 33 years of service, particularly during my tenure as Chief. In Birmingham, we shared moments of triumph, like achieving the lowest homicide totals in nearly half a century, record lows in other categories and earning recognition as a model agency while spearheading nationwide initiatives in community engagement and reconciliation. These endeavors underscored a vital truth: that it was possible to simultaneously reduce crime and nurture trust within the community.

Of course, there were arduous challenges, but in the grand tapestry of our experiences, they pale in comparison to the profound connections forged during quieter moments. There's nothing quite like sitting on a grandmother's porch, engaging in heartfelt conversations about life. Or the joy of a father bounding into his home, eagerly summoning the entire family outside for a cherished photo with "His" Chief. It was effortless for me to establish these connections because, at some point in my life, I had called each of the four police precincts home. I knew the streets intimately, but more importantly, I knew and held deep respect for the people who called those streets their own.

I want to extend a heartfelt "shout out" to every dedicated law enforcement officer and support staff member who tirelessly serve our communities. I must also recognize the unsung heroes in this endeavor, the families who stand as the real MVPs. My wife grew accustomed to the sound of Velcro awakening her in the dead of night, for that unmistakable noise signaled my safe return home, the shedding of a bullet-proof vest, and a moment of respite.

In these turbulent and uncertain times, I implore all law enforcement officers to uphold their solemn oath and to stand unwaveringly against those who would betray it. Keep your honor pristine, and above all, stay safe. Your families and the communities you serve rely on your unwavering commitment to ensure you return home safely after each shift, forging bonds that stand as a testament to the strength of your service. Methods may change but values should be beyond reproach.

Leading Change

Change is essential for organizations to adapt, innovate, grow, and thrive in a constantly evolving world. It is a catalyst for progress and a means of staying competitive, relevant, and responsive to the needs of customers, employees, and society at large.

The advent of artificial intelligence (AI), machine learning (ML), robotics and quantum computing represents a transformative era that demands leaders who are forward-thinking, adaptable, and capable of navigating the complexities and opportunities presented by these innovations. It is not merely about adopting new tools; it's about leading organizations through a profound shift in how business is conducted, products and services are delivered, and relationships with citizens, customers and employees are managed.

In today's digital age, we are inundated with an overwhelming amount of information, easily accessible at our fingertips. However, the availability of information doesn't guarantee success in achieving our goals of financial prosperity, physical well-being, or fulfilling relationships.

Many of us mistakenly believe that simply gathering more information will automatically lead to progress. We fail to recognize that while information is abundant and often freely available, taking meaningful action requires effort, determination, and sometimes risk.

Therefore, instead of solely focusing on amassing more knowledge, it's essential to understand that the real challenge lies in turning that information into practical steps and decisions that propel us forward. By taking deliberate and consistent actions based on the information we already have, we can make meaningful progress towards our objectives.

Through my extensive experiences, the paramount lesson that has crystallized is that effective leaders must excel in two critical domains. First and foremost, leaders must master the art of "painting the target." To draw a clear analogy, think of a laser marking a target with a distinctive heat signature. This signature serves as the guiding light, directing a projectile weapon to precisely strike that marked point. In essence, painting the target signifies the act of spotlighting the problem, bringing it into sharp focus, so it can be eradicated.

However, a pervasive challenge observed in change management is a deviation from this principle. Leaders, in their eagerness to usher in solutions, tend to illuminate the resolution when many individuals within the organization are ensconced in their comfort zones. This approach often results in dismal failure as the majority fail to perceive any problem worth solving. Consequently, they instinctively resist the proposed changes, which are seen as solutions to non-existent issues. This resistance not only hinders progress but also fosters a pervasive aversion to the very notion of change. Thus, the critical lesson lies in the need for leaders to first highlight the problem before unveiling the solution, ensuring that the path to change is one illuminated by necessity rather than imposition.

> **For successful change management, leaders must highlight the problem.**

William Bridges in his book, *Managing Transition: Making the Most of Change* explains the reason most change agents fail is because they focus on the solution instead of the problem. He sells the point that leaders should spend 90% of their effort selling the problem and helping people understand what is "not" working.[49] I agree with his premise that people won't accept a solution when they never perceived a problem so in essence, leaders must define reality.

My second pivotal revelation underscores the necessity for leaders to embrace the practice of relentless over-communication. In the intricate dance of change, it's essential to recognize that the onus of guiding this transformation squarely rests on the shoulders of the leader. While we fervently seek the buy-in, support, and acceptance of those embarking on this journey, the ultimate responsibility for success lies with the leader.

Thus, it falls upon the leader to meticulously craft a communication strategy tailored to each individual involved in the change process. This bespoke plan must serve as a beacon, shedding light on the crucial information that individuals need to assimilate, comprehend, and appreciate the essence of the change and its profound significance. The voids left by inadequate communication inevitably become fertile ground for rumors and innuendos, which, like weeds, swiftly proliferate with falsehoods that obscure the truth. Therefore, the leader's role as the purveyor of accurate and relevant information is not only pivotal but also the linchpin for the success of the entire change initiative.

Change agents must remember any information gaps will be filled by rumors and innuendos.

In the ever-evolving landscape of organizational development and improvement, one fundamental truth remains abundantly clear: "one and done" training events or team engagements, despite their initial appeal, frequently fall short in their capacity to deliver substantial and lasting change. They may serve as a brief spark of inspiration or knowledge infusion, but when it comes to the long-term cultivation of a healthy and purpose-driven workplace culture, or team dynamics they are often insufficient.

To comprehend why these isolated interventions are inadequate for achieving sustained transformation, we must first consider the nature of culture and change within an organization. Culture is not a static entity; it is a living, breathing force that shapes the attitudes, behaviors, and values of a collective. Changing it, especially for the better, is akin to altering the course of a river—it demands persistent effort, gradual adjustments, and a deep understanding of the currents that influence its flow.

Imagine a scenario where a company decides to address communication issues within its teams by conducting a one-day communication skills workshop. The workshop may indeed provide some valuable insights and tools, and participants may leave feeling motivated to apply what they've learned. However, without ongoing reinforcement, follow-up, and integration of these newfound skills into the daily work environment, the initial enthusiasm tends to fade, and old habits resurface.

Furthermore, "one and done" initiatives often lack the depth and customization needed to address an organization's unique challenges adequately. Organizational cultures are like fingerprints—no two are exactly alike. Therefore, a cookie-cutter approach to training and engagement is unlikely to resonate with the specific needs, values, and intricacies of a given workplace. Achieving clarity and purpose in organizational culture requires tailored solutions that align with the company's mission, vision, and distinct identity.

Consider, for instance, an organization that aspires to instill a culture of innovation. Hosting a single brainstorming session or innovation workshop might spark creativity momentarily, but without a sustained effort to nurture and institutionalize innovative thinking, it remains a fleeting moment rather than a lasting culture. True clarity of purpose in this context necessitates an ongoing commitment to fostering innovation, including dedicated resources, a supportive infrastructure, and continuous encouragement.

Moreover, the journey towards enduring change and a purpose-driven culture involves not only knowledge acquisition but also behavioral transformation. Individuals within an organization must not only understand the desired values and principles but also internalize and practice them consistently. This depth of transformation requires time, repetition, and guidance that is typically lacking in one-off events.

In contrast, organizations that commit to a long-term strategy of cultural development and change recognize the value of continuous learning and reinforcement. They understand that culture is not a destination but a journey. To achieve clarity of purpose and a culture aligned with their values, they implement multi-faceted, ongoing initiatives.

These initiatives might include regular training sessions, mentorship programs, leadership development, and a commitment to open communication. They encourage feedback loops, allowing employees to contribute to the evolution of the culture. Such organizations are more likely to succeed in their quest for a purpose-driven culture because they invest in the long-term cultivation of desired behaviors, values, and attitudes.

Achieving clarity of purpose, which is having a clear understanding of why we exist and what we aim to achieve, and lasting change requires a commitment to continuous, tailored initiatives that focus on behavior and align with an organization's unique identity and goals. Culture change is not a quick fix; it's a continuous journey that requires dedication and patience. Only through persistent effort can organizations truly navigate the currents of culture and steer them toward a brighter and more purposeful destination.

Another key to change is understanding the importance of timing. Timing is important in every aspect of life. In the military we say executing an 80% plan on time is better than executing a 100% plan too late. Timing is also critical in regards to personal development. What was impossible at some time in the past may be possible now or even later as you develop these seven essentials. Quite often challenges and issues that looked formidable in the past become much simpler later in life. It can be a matter of skills, experiences, resources, or even perspective.

We also see the importance of timing in business and corporate-ship. In a strategic move showcasing impeccable timing, Apple Inc. navigated a critical decision that propelled its success. Analyzing market trends and consumer behaviors, Apple identified a unique window of opportunity to launch the iPhone, a groundbreaking product that revolutionized the smartphone industry. Leveraging this temporal advantage, they aligned their innovation with the evolving needs of the target audience, capturing attention and market share. This well-timed decision not only demonstrated Apple's astute business acumen but also solidified the company's position as an industry leader. The strategic insight gained from this experience is reminiscent of the principles discussed in works such as *Good Strategy Bad Strategy: The Difference and Why it Matters* by Richard Rumelt, emphasizing the importance of aligning actions with a keen understanding of the temporal landscape in business[50].

In another telecommunications example regarding timing but related to the policing landscape, in May 2020, Google was planning to unveil new Android 11 features but decided to delay the unveiling due to national demonstrations and riots resulting from the death of George Floyd at the hand of a Minneapolis Police Officer. A tweet said "We are excited to tell you more about Android 11, but now is not the time to celebrate." Google says that it will "be back with more on Android 11, soon," but at that time, did not advise when that might be.[51]

Whether it was good corporate citizenship or totally driven by capitalism, Google decision makers understood the importance of timing as our nation continues to grapple with issues like racism, climate impacts, globalization, and poverty to name just a few. Although the greatest nation on earth, these remain major societal challenges with no end in sight; also known as "wicked problems."

Wicked Problems

"Wicked problems", often referred to as complex problems, present an intricate web of challenges that defy straightforward solutions. These issues are characterized by several key factors that make them particularly difficult to address effectively.

Firstly, "wicked problems" are plagued by incomplete, contradictory, and constantly evolving requirements. Unlike well-defined problems with clear parameters and solutions, the parameters of wicked problems are often elusive and subject to change. This inherent ambiguity makes it challenging to even identify the scope of the problem, let alone formulate a definitive solution.

Secondly, "wicked problems" are notorious for involving a multitude of stakeholders, each with their own perspectives, interests, and opinions. This diversity of viewpoints can lead to conflicts, power struggles, and competing priorities, further complicating the problem-solving process. The sheer number of people involved can also make it difficult to coordinate efforts and reach consensus.

Moreover, "wicked problems" rarely exist in isolation. They are deeply interconnected with other problems, creating a complex web of dependencies. Attempting to solve a "wicked problem" in isolation can inadvertently exacerbate other issues or create unintended consequences elsewhere. This interconnectivity adds another layer of complexity to the already intricate nature of these problems.

It's crucial to note that the term wicked does not imply malevolence but rather resistance to resolution. "Wicked problems" are named as such because they resist conventional problem-solving methods and often lack clear-cut solutions. They challenge our traditional problem-solving approaches and demand innovative, adaptive, and collaborative strategies.

Addressing "wicked problems" requires a holistic approach that acknowledges their complexity, embraces uncertainty, and involves diverse stakeholders in a collaborative effort. It necessitates continuous learning, adaptation, and a willingness to accept that complete resolution may be elusive. While "wicked problems" may never be entirely solved, progress can be made through ongoing efforts to mitigate their impacts and improve the systems in which they arise.

The inherent complexity of "wicked problems" is evident in their multifaceted nature, making them far beyond the scope of any single individual or organization to tackle in isolation. To effectively address these formidable challenges, a fundamental shift is required—a shift towards collaboration among teams of individuals and organizations, united by a shared vision and purpose. These teams must be willing to break down the imaginary lines that often divide us, recognizing that the solutions to these complex issues lie at the intersection of various perspectives and expertise.

An example of this collaborative approach and shared vision occurred during "Operation Allies Welcome" in 2021. This was a massive effort that resettled over 70,000 Afghan refugees in the United States. These individuals had risked their lives to support our military efforts, and when the time came, it was our duty to ensure their safe transition to a new life.

Having deployed and served in Afghanistan, I understood firsthand the sacrifices they had made. But understanding their struggle was not enough. We had to act, and we had to do so in the face of constantly shifting realities. Our team coordinated everything from housing and medical care to education and job training. Initially, we were told to prepare for 3,000 Afghans in a single location. That plan didn't last long. Before we knew it, we weren't just managing a single resettlement site. We were building and sustaining eight fully functioning communities for nearly 80,000 people.

Managing this level of change required flexibility, strategic thinking, and an unwavering commitment to the mission. We had to shift from a linear mindset to an adaptive one, moving from reacting to anticipating. What worked at one site didn't necessarily work at another. Resources were stretched, timelines were unpredictable, and the pressure to get it right was enormous. But we didn't have the luxury of waiting for perfect conditions. We had to make critical decisions in real time, knowing that lives depended on our ability to lead through uncertainty.

This experience underscored a powerful lesson about managing change. Plans will shift, conditions will evolve, and expectations will be redefined. True leadership embraces uncertainty, stays mission-focused, and finds solutions in the face of adversity. Change, especially on this scale, can feel overwhelming, but by remaining agile, working collaboratively, and keeping our purpose at the forefront, we were able to turn chaos into coordinated action.

My law enforcement experience was crucial in this operation. It helped me ask the right questions from my position of perspective, understand why Homeowners Associations (HOAs) and neighborhood groups would be concerned, and recognize the importance of Crime Prevention Through Environmental Design (CPTED). The way we constructed and laid out each small Afghan city had a direct impact on safety, security, and public perception.

As a Police Chief, I made it a point to walk through the neighborhoods we served, not just during the good times, but during the challenging moments as well. I approached the Afghan communities the same way, walking through them with a translator, listening, observing, and ensuring that the environment fostered both security and dignity.

However, this operation was limited in time and specific in scope. There's an even greater challenge when creating lasting change. In the truest sense of the term, this entails implementing substantial and transformative shifts that drive genuine progress in our society. These changes go beyond superficial adjustments and instead, reshape the very foundations of our systems, policies, and practices. However, the path to such enduring transformation remains elusive unless we, as a society, collectively embrace change as a catalyst for progress. After all, success leads to remarkable achievements, while failure offers profound insights. In either scenario, greatness emerges.

This embracement of change is not merely a passive acceptance but an active and deliberate choice. It involves recognizing that the status quo may no longer serve us and that our willingness to adapt and evolve is paramount. Embracing change requires a shift in mindset, where we view challenges as opportunities for growth and innovation rather than obstacles to be avoided. It entails a commitment to continuous learning, flexibility, and an openness to new ideas and approaches.

> **Embracing change requires a shift in mindset, where we view challenges as opportunities for growth and innovation rather than obstacles to be avoided.**

Crossing the bridge towards resolution of "wicked problems" is not a one-time event but an ongoing journey. It requires dedication, persistence, and a shared commitment to the betterment of our society. By coming together in collaborative efforts, we can harness the collective intelligence, creativity, and resources needed to address these complex challenges. In doing so, we move closer to realizing lasting change that leaves a positive and enduring impact in our personal lives, on our communities and the world at large. Status Quo isn't good enough... **Embrace Change.**

Reflective Questions for Chapter 7

Change is inevitable, but your response to it defines your growth as a leader. The questions below encourage you to think about how you embrace, lead, and navigate change in your life. Are you resilient in the face of uncertainty? Do you proactively seek out opportunities for transformation? Reflect on your adaptability and willingness to step out of your comfort zone to drive positive change for yourself and those you lead.

1. Think about a time when you resisted change in your personal or professional life. What were the underlying fears or concerns, and how did the change ultimately impact you?

2. What aspects of your life or work feel stagnant? How could embracing change, even if it's uncomfortable, open up new possibilities for growth and progress?

3. When faced with a significant change, do you typically embrace, comply, tolerate, or resist? How can you shift your mindset to be more open to the opportunities that change presents?

4. Reflect on a change you successfully navigated. What strategies did you use to adapt, and how can those lessons guide you in future changes?

5. How do you respond to critics or resistors of change, both in yourself and others? What steps can you take to better manage criticism and foster a more positive attitude toward change in your personal and professional circles?

Epilogue: The Gift of Legacy

> "The things you do for yourself are gone when you are gone, but the things you do for others remain as your legacy."[52]
>
> - Kalu Ndukwe Kalu

ON A CHILLY, SNOW-DRAPED EVENING, as I was preparing to leave the sprawling complex of the Pentagon, a particular sight caught my attention. There, amidst the descending snowflakes, I spotted an elegantly dressed, older gentleman diligently pushing a cart through the parking lot. The cart bore the weight of what appeared to be a trove of gifts and mementos, leading me to deduce that this man had just concluded a long and distinguished career, perhaps marking his retirement. Intrigued, I followed him to his vehicle, arriving just as he popped open the trunk.

Stepping forward, I introduced myself, and I could sense the surprise in his eyes at the unexpected assistance from a General Officer. This chance encounter provided me with the perfect opportunity to engage in conversation, not merely about the logistics of his big day but also to extend my heartfelt gratitude for his many years of dedicated service. As he fought back his emotions, he nodded appreciatively, and with his vehicle now loaded, he embarked on the next chapter of his life.

Watching him drive away, I couldn't help but contemplate the notion of leaving a legacy. For some, it might manifest in the memorabilia they take with them, tangible reminders of their career's accomplishments. However, I have always believed that success is not found in the gifts one carries away but in the lasting gift of legacy one leaves behind.

As I glanced back at the Pentagon, its lights still ablaze, and vehicles dotting the parking lot, it struck me that the mission never truly ends. It continues with renewed vigor, carried forward by those who remain within those hallowed halls. In that moment, I fervently hoped that this retiring gentleman had left a lasting impact on the lives of his colleagues and subordinates, that they would remember him not for the trinkets he carried away, but for the inspiration, guidance, and wisdom he had imparted. After all, a legacy isn't etched in memorabilia; it's etched in hearts and minds, enduring long after one has departed the stage.

Living the Legacy

My official name is A.C. Roper, Jr. Of course, throughout my life people would ask, "What does A.C. stand for?" Depending on my age, I had a different response. As a kid, I would say, "nothing" or it doesn't stand for anything. As a teenager, thinking I was cool, I would respond Al Capone or some other imaginary name. It was similar to the "G" in Fred G. Sanford from the old Sanford and Son television series starring Red Foxx. It would stand for different things totally based on who was asking and the scenario. In the end, I would often surrender and say "I'm a junior and my Dad's name is A.C. Sr."

My mother, Shirley Roper was the epitome of grace, style and resilience. During my parents' early days in Detroit, she counted the stars of Motown as friends and in some inexplicable way, even traveled with them. Whenever my mother watched Motown anniversary videos, she'd reminisce about hanging out with the stars. She'd share stories of dancing with Smoky Robinson, noting how his eye color resembled my Dad's. The Temptations, Diana Ross, and the Supremes were all part of those memories. Although I never heard her sing, Mom might have fit right in with the Supremes. If she could chime in now, she'd probably insist on being Diana, envisioning the group as Shirley and the Supremes — a name that seems to suit them better.

My Dad was a good man and when he died on Christmas Day in 2018 I lost a friend. He believed in chasing your dreams no matter how stacked the odds were against you. He was in his late 60's when during a phone call he casually mentioned he wanted to learn about computers. So, unsurprisingly, he began attending computer classes at a community college. He would camp out in front of YouTube videos and before long he was buying broken laptops at the local thrift stores for less than $20.00. He would take them home, diagnose the problem, buy the low-cost replacement part on-line and repair the computer. His hobby resulted in him gifting his grandkids with laptop computers.

A.C. Sr. was a gifted man but never served in uniform. However, as a young man he marched in the streets of Birmingham fighting for civil rights. In essence he was a "Foot Soldier" but not an Army Soldier. His Big Brother, my Uncle AL was the Army Soldier. An Airborne Special Forces Officer who served in Vietnam and Korea, he motivated me and inspired my life of service. I was honored to speak at his funeral service and render a final salute. Their father, my Granddad, William Roper served during World War I. He deployed to France as a Buffalo Soldier with Company

F, 366th Infantry, 92nd Infantry Division. According to the World War I Memorial in Washington DC, unlike many segregated units assigned menial support roles, the 92nd Division saw active combat in France.

Corporal William Roper fought in the Meuse-Argonne Campaign which, according to the Memorial, was the largest battle in American history. The U.S. and its Allies prevailed but 26,000 American soldiers died during the battle. Granddad survived but was gassed on September 1, 1918, and again on November 11, 1918, the last day of the war on what was referred to as "Armistice Day" which is now our "Veterans' Day." His discharge papers say, "Character: Excellent." Granddad didn't leave some large estate, but he left us a legacy of excellence, character and honor!

Granddad emerged from the shadows of the original Buffalo Soldiers, casting a profound legacy for those, like me, who would follow in their footsteps. The tale of the Buffalo Soldiers stands as an extraordinary chapter in American history, marked by unwavering resilience, unflinching bravery, and an unwavering commitment to duty in the face of insurmountable challenges. The term "Buffalo Soldiers" was first bestowed upon them by Native American tribes, who drew parallels between these African American troops and the revered buffalo, recognizing their shared strength and distinctive dark, curly hair. Comprising former slaves, freemen, and Black Civil War veterans, these soldiers voluntarily enlisted in the U.S. Army post-Civil War. Predominantly of African American descent, they played a pivotal role not only in the western frontier but also in shaping the nation's destiny, leaving an indelible mark that continues to resonate with me and countless others.

In the grand scheme of life, success is often measured by the mark we leave on the world. This mark extends far beyond professional achievements or material possessions; it's about the lives we touch and the positive influence we exert. Legacy leaders understand that their true impact lies not only in the results they produce but also in the relationships they cultivate.

Leaving a Legacy

Your legacy transcends the confines of effective leadership or the attainment of individual objectives. It encompasses something far more profound: the enduring impact you leave on others through the example you set and the inspiration you ignite within them. This legacy is a catalyst that propels individuals to venture beyond their comfort zones, ushering in personal growth that ripples outward to touch not only their lives but also those of their families and communities. In fact, the transformative power of such inspiration can extend through generations, becoming a beacon of positive change for years to come.

Taking a moment to reflect on the profound practice of mentoring and nurturing the growth of others is a fundamental pillar of both personal and professional development. In the whirlwind of our own aspirations and goals, it's easy to lose sight of the fact that genuine success extends far beyond personal accomplishments. True achievement is intrinsically linked to the impact we have on those around us and the legacy we cultivate.

The fallacy of selfishness can confine our perspective, leading us to believe that the pursuit of success is a solitary venture. However, the truth lies in the profound fulfillment that emanates from helping others thrive alongside us. Mentoring and guiding others is a way of repaying the debt of knowledge, experiences, and opportunities that we have received on our own life journey.

Foremost in this intricate dance is the role of the mentor. A mentor stands as a compass, offering invaluable insights, wisdom, and unwavering support to navigate the intricate landscapes of life and career. They grant us access to a broader perspective, share their own experiences, and bestow upon us constructive feedback that accelerates our personal and professional growth.

Equally vital is the mantle of being a mentor to someone else. Mentoring transcends the boundaries of mere transaction; it's about contribution. When we take on the role of a mentor, we actively contribute to the growth and success of others. We assist them in traversing their own hurdles, provide guidance, and share the wealth of our own knowledge. In this role, we become an integral part of their journey towards accomplishment, leaving an indelible imprint on their lives.

The conviction that every individual should both have a mentor and be a mentor underscores the profound reciprocity of growth. Seeking guidance from someone with more experience not only accelerates our progress but also allows us to avoid the pitfalls they have previously navigated. Simultaneously, mentoring someone else empowers us to solidify our own understanding, refine our communication skills, and play an influential role in another person's trajectory.

This dual path of mentorship and learning is the essence of what I refer to as a "Legacy Line" or "Leadership Wake." It signifies that the knowledge and values we transmit to those we mentor continue to ripple through generations, forming an enduring legacy.

The act of mentoring and being mentored exceeds mere altruism; it's a potent strategy for personal growth and a means of crafting a profound legacy. It strengthens our bonds with others, fosters a culture of perpetual learning, and guarantees that our impact persists long after we've achieved our individual objectives. In essence, it means that the organizations we touch should be improved because we were there, but more profoundly, someone's life should be markedly better for having crossed our path. It is the embodiment of a legacy that transcends time and elevates the human experience.

It is crucial to draw a distinction between mentorship and sponsorship in this context. While the mantle of mentorship is one you extend readily to anyone seeking guidance and growth, sponsorship is a different matter altogether. It is a deeper commitment, one bestowed upon those whose values and character align closely with the principles and ideals you hold dear. Sponsorship entails not only guiding someone's journey but also vouching for them, investing your reputation and influence in their success, and entrusting them to carry forward the legacy you've built. It is a bond of trust and shared purpose, representing a mutual commitment to upholding and perpetuating the values that define your legacy.

Consider the concept of a "Legacy Tree." Just as a tree extends its branches to provide shade, shelter, and sustenance, legacy leaders extend their influence to nurture and support those around them. As an old Greek proverb states, legacy leaders "plant trees whose shade they will never see." These leaders understand that their actions today shape the future, much like planting seeds that grow into mighty oaks.

Moreover, legacy leaders understand the importance of recognizing potential in everyone, regardless of their current circumstances. Those who execute duties of their leadership position without making potential appreciation and cultivation paramount do not steward their team well. This is antithetical to enduring influence and incompatible with legacy leadership. Nonetheless, leaders who do see and celebrate team members' potential are the ante-dote for those who are not legacy-minded. They inspire the achievement of higher heights and just as my former supervisor's laughter failed to deter my leadership development, legacy leaders shine a light that guides past would — be obstacles on the journey to success.

Legacy leaders understand that success is more than just numbers on a balance sheet or achievements on a resume. It's about the lives they touch, the relationships they build, and the positive influence they exert on others. Neglecting relationships, whether intentionally or inadvertently, can lead to a legacy tainted by broken bonds, unfulfilled potential, and missed opportunities.

In 2022, I had the distinct honor of hosting a retirement ceremony in honor of Army Reserve Chief Warrant Officer 5 (CW5) Phillip Brashear. These types of events are outstanding opportunities to reflect on what's important in life — I'm talking about service and legacy — and I can't think of a better example than Chief Brashear and his family. Chief Brashear has served our nation in multiple capacities and military components for almost 40 years!

I doubt there is any service member who is not aware of the amazing life and career of Phillip's father, Navy Master Chief Carl Brashear as played by Cuba Gooding, Jr in the movie, "Men of Honor." Truly inspiring! This multi-generational legacy is something to marvel — to think of the adversity those before us had to face, the barriers they had to tear down, and the fruits that their efforts have born — it's truly amazing and humbling to me.

Often when you think about legacy, it's something that is left behind after a person has passed. Legacy extends beyond the accumulation of material wealth; it's about imparting the wisdom gained, sharing values, and passing down knowledge rather than just possessions or earnings. In other words, legacy means values more than valuables and wisdom over wealth (Given that material wealth constitutes only a tiny fraction of your legacy). A more comprehensive understanding of legacy emerges when one finds true purpose in dedicating themselves to making a profound, enduring, and inspiring impact on humanity by wholeheartedly serving a cause larger than their individual self.

We've all seen the negative examples that serve as stark reminders that true success is a delicate balance between achieving personal goals and valuing the people who contribute to those achievements. Legacy leaders learn from these cautionary tales, recognizing that nurturing relationships is not just a soft skill, but a fundamental aspect of leaving a positive and enduring legacy. By avoiding the pitfalls of neglecting relationships, they create a legacy that shines brightly and positively impacts generations to come.

A legacy, in its essence, is not a testament to vanity or a fleeting desire for recognition. It is, instead, an embodiment of our core values, the imprints of our actions, and the echo of our influence. It is the indelible signature we inscribe upon the world, resonating through the corridors of history and guiding the moral compass of future generations. It is a measure of the lives we've touched, the inspiration we've ignited, and the positive change we've imparted.

Before the end, whether that marks the closing of a life, the conclusion of an illustrious career, or the transition from one role to another, we are called upon to consider our legacy. To embark on this introspective journey is to confront the question: What do we wish to be remembered for?

This question is not confined to the realm of philosophy or self-indulgence; it is a beacon that illuminates the path of our actions and decisions. By contemplating the legacy we aim to create, we are equipped with a roadmap to navigate the labyrinth of life's choices. It urges us to question the motives behind our actions, the intentions that drive our pursuits, and the values we uphold in our daily interactions.

As we traverse the corridors of existence, our legacy is intricately interwoven with the lives we touch. It finds expression in the kindness we extend to strangers, the mentorship we offer to colleagues, and the wisdom we impart to the next generation. It is in these seemingly ordinary moments that the extraordinary power of legacy takes root. It is the hope of leaving the world a better place than we found it, of being a positive force in the lives of others.

Consider the legacy of a dedicated teacher who imparts knowledge, not merely for the sake of academic achievement but to inspire a lifelong love of learning in their students. Or the legacy of a compassionate healthcare worker who brings comfort to those in pain, not just through medical expertise but through a genuine and caring presence. These legacies are not measured in wealth or accolades; they are etched in the hearts and minds of those whose lives were touched.

As we delve deeper into the intricate tapestry of legacy, we discover that it is a reflection of our values and principles. It is the embodiment of the ethical compass that guides our decisions. For some, legacy may be synonymous with social justice, the tireless pursuit of equality, and the dismantling of systemic inequities. For others, it may be the preservation of nature and the commitment to environmental stewardship.

It encompasses the relationships we cultivate, the communities we nurture, and the bonds we strengthen. It is the legacy of a loving parent who instills the values of empathy and kindness in their children, knowing that these principles will be carried forward into the future. It is the legacy of a collaborative team that, through shared vision and dedication, achieves feats greater than the sum of its parts. The legacy we aspire to create reflects the ideals we hold dear and I recognize for some, it is strictly financial or other types of economic prosperity.

In the context of a professional career, the notion of legacy takes on a unique significance. It is not limited to the attainment of personal success but extends to the cultivation of a positive and enduring impact within an organization. Consider the visionary leader who, in addition to achieving business goals, fosters a culture of innovation and empowers employees to realize their potential. Their legacy is not confined to the bottom line; it is woven into the very fabric of the company's identity.

Conversely, the absence of a considered legacy can lead to a career marked by aimless pursuits and transient achievements. Without a guiding star, one may find themselves adrift in a sea of short-term objectives, disconnected from a deeper sense of purpose. It is in these moments of reflection that we may grapple with questions of meaning and fulfillment, seeking a more profound sense of direction.

To embark on a deliberate path of legacy is to imbue one's actions with intentionality. It is to align our daily choices with a broader vision of the impact we wish to create. By setting our sights on a meaningful legacy, we are propelled to transcend the constraints of immediate gratification and short-lived successes. Instead, we invest in endeavors that contribute to the greater good and stand the test of time.

Yet, the pursuit of legacy is not without its challenges. It demands courage in the face of adversity, an unwavering commitment to principles, and a willingness to confront the inevitable setbacks along the way. It calls for courage in the pursuit of justice, compassion in the face of suffering, and empathy in understanding the diverse perspectives of others. It requires us to navigate the complexities of a changing world while remaining steadfast in our values.

At the heart of this profound endeavor are two essential elements: resiliency and self-care. These intertwined qualities not only sustain individuals through life's challenges but also ensure that their contributions remain meaningful and enduring.

Resiliency is the ability to recover from setbacks and adapt to changing circumstances. It's the inner strength that propels you forward, even in the face of adversity. This quality is crucial for leaving a legacy because the path to significant accomplishments is often fraught with obstacles. Without resilience, one may falter when confronted with difficulties, potentially leaving goals unfulfilled. Resiliency allows you to persist through hardship, continually striving toward your vision. It also sets an example for others, demonstrating that perseverance and determination can overcome even the most daunting challenges. In this way, resiliency not only aids in achieving personal goals but also inspires and empowers future generations to face their own trials with courage and fortitude.

Self-care, on the other hand, is the practice of taking deliberate actions to maintain physical, mental, and emotional well-being. In the quest to leave a legacy, it is easy to become consumed by the demands and pressures of ambition. However, neglecting self-care can lead to burnout, reduced effectiveness, and ultimately, an inability to sustain the effort required to make a lasting impact. Prioritizing self-care ensures that you remain healthy, focused, and energized. This holistic approach to well-being enables continuous contribution and innovation, as a well-cared-for mind and body are more capable of creative thinking and problem-solving.

Furthermore, self-care embodies the principle of leading by example. When you prioritize your own well-being, you demonstrate the importance of balance and self-respect to those around you. This influence can be particularly significant for those in leadership positions or roles that involve mentoring others. By modeling self-care, leaders encourage their peers and successors to value their own health and well-being, fostering a culture that supports sustained effort and long-term success.

Integrating resiliency and self-care also cultivates a positive environment conducive to collective growth. Resilient individuals who practice self-care are better equipped to support others, creating a ripple effect that extends their influence. They can offer guidance, encouragement, and a sense of stability, contributing to a community that values mutual support and shared resilience. This nurturing atmosphere not only enhances individual contributions but also strengthens the collective legacy of the group.

Ultimately, the importance of resiliency and self-care in leaving a legacy cannot be overstated. These qualities ensure that you can navigate the inevitable challenges you will encounter, maintain your well-being, and continue to contribute meaningfully over the long term. By embodying resilience and practicing self-care, you not only achieve personal success but also inspire others to pursue their own legacies with strength and compassion. This holistic approach to legacy-building creates a lasting impact that transcends individual accomplishments, fostering a world where resilience and well-being are valued and nurtured for generations to come.

To paraphrase a famous pop song, we must start with the person in the mirror and I submit that legacy is the mirror that reflects the essence of our character and the trajectory of our influence. It is a reminder that our actions, no matter how small or seemingly insignificant, have a cumulative impact on the world. It prompts us to recognize that the choices we make today ripple through time, shaping the world of tomorrow.

To consider one's legacy is to embark on a journey of self-discovery and introspection. It is a call to transcend the transient and the ephemeral, reaching for the enduring and the meaningful. It is an invitation to be architects of positive change, craftsmen of a better world, and stewards of the values we hold dear.

In conclusion, the notion of legacy is not a distant concern reserved for the end of life's narrative. It is a guiding star that illuminates our path, a compass that directs our choices, and a tapestry woven with the threads of our values. It is the mark we leave on the world, the influence we wield, and the echo of our existence. By considering our legacy, we embark on a profound and transformative journey, one that shapes not only our own destiny but also the destiny of the world we leave behind.

In essence, legacy leaders understand that their influence extends far beyond their own lifetimes. They recognize that by adhering to these seven foundational principles: nurturing relationships, honoring humility, guarding integrity, practicing discipline, cultivating excellence, building partnerships, and embracing change, they are sowing the seeds of a legacy that will continue to flourish, providing shade and sustenance to generations yet to come. Wherever you stand in life today, remember this: in the grand scheme of things, it is never too late to embrace the greatest gift you can offer the future, The *Gift of Legacy*. Live with *No Limits!*

Seven Keys to Life, Legacy, and Leadership:

A Daily Focus Guide

The journey to becoming a transformative leader doesn't happen overnight. It requires intentional focus and daily practice of the key principles that define who you are and how you lead. This guide is structured to provide a daily focus, allowing you to deepen your understanding and application of the seven keys to life, legacy, and leadership presented in this book. Use it as a roadmap to enrich your personal growth, strengthen your leadership approach, and amplify your impact.

Monday: Integrity

Kickstart your week with a focus on integrity. Integrity is the cornerstone of trust and credibility. It means doing what's right, even when no one is watching, and upholding your values under pressure. Today, reflect on your actions and ensure they align with your principles. Integrity is not just about big decisions but also about the small, everyday choices that define your character.

- Reflection Question: What is one action I can take today to ensure my words and deeds align with my core values?

- Action Step: Identify a recent situation where your integrity was tested, and consider how you handled it. What did you learn, and how can you strengthen your commitment to integrity moving forward?

Tuesday: Discipline

On Tuesday, cultivate discipline—the force that drives you to take consistent action toward your goals. Discipline isn't about restriction but about freeing yourself to pursue what truly matters with focus and determination. Today, set a clear intention and follow through, even if distractions or obstacles arise.

- Reflection Question: How can I improve my daily habits to stay disciplined in the pursuit of my goals?
- Action Step: Choose a habit you want to reinforce or establish today, such as setting aside uninterrupted time for deep work, prioritizing health, or maintaining consistent communication with your team.

Wednesday: Excellence

Midweek, dedicate yourself to the pursuit of excellence. Excellence is not about perfection but about striving to go beyond what's required. It's about raising the standard for yourself and inspiring those around you to do the same. Challenge yourself to deliver your best work, no matter the task.

- Reflection Question: What can I do today to go above and beyond in my responsibilities?
- Action Step: Identify one area in your personal or professional life where you can elevate your performance, and take deliberate steps to achieve a higher level of excellence.

Thursday: Relationships

Relationships are the foundation of both personal fulfillment and effective leadership. Today, focus on nurturing your relationships—whether at work or at home. Strong relationships are built on trust, respect, and meaningful interactions. Take the time to connect authentically with those around you and invest in the people who matter most.

- Reflection Question: How can I show appreciation and support to someone in my life today?

- Action Step: Reach out to a colleague, friend, or family member and express gratitude or offer your help. Strengthen your bond by engaging in an open and genuine conversation.

Friday: Humility

End the workweek with a focus on humility. Humility is recognizing that every person has something valuable to contribute. It's about being open to learning, admitting mistakes, and giving credit where it's due. Humility strengthens your leadership by fostering a culture of respect and collaboration.

- Reflection Question: How can I demonstrate humility today in a way that uplifts others and encourages openness?

- Action Step: Seek feedback on a recent decision or project and truly listen to the insights offered. Let those around you know that their perspectives are valued.

Saturday: Partnerships

Dedicate Saturday to evaluating and nurturing your partnerships. Partnerships—whether in business, community, or personal life—are key to achieving greater impact and shared success. Reflect on the quality of your partnerships and consider ways to build stronger alliances based on mutual trust and shared goals.

- Reflection Question: What steps can I take today to strengthen a current partnership or establish a new one?

- Action Step: Reach out to a potential or existing partner, share your vision, and discuss ways to collaborate for mutual benefit.

Sunday: Change

Close the week by embracing change as an opportunity for growth. Change can be unsettling, but it's also a catalyst for progress. Today, focus on your attitude towards change and how you can become more adaptable and proactive in managing transitions, both big and small.

- Reflection Question: How can I approach upcoming changes with a positive mindset and lead others through uncertainty?

- Action Step: Identify a change you want to initiate in your life, whether personal or professional, and outline the first steps you will take to make it happen.

By dedicating each day to one of these seven keys, you will reinforce the principles that underpin effective leadership and personal growth. This daily guide is a tool to help you stay aligned with your values and continually develop the mindset and habits needed to create a lasting legacy of excellence, integrity, and service.

Appendix A: The Cascading Power of Consistency

Consistency is a cornerstone of living a life of discipline, and its importance cannot be overstated. It serves as the glue that binds our intentions and actions, transforming our goals into tangible realities. Here's why consistency is crucial in maintaining a disciplined life:

1. **Establishing Habits**: Consistency is the key to forming and maintaining positive habits. When you consistently engage in a behavior or routine, it becomes ingrained in your daily life. Discipline relies on habitual actions that align with your goals, whether they involve health, productivity, or personal development. These habits become second nature, making it easier to stay on track.

2. **Building Momentum**: Consistency generates momentum. Just as a rolling snowball gathers more snow as it moves, your efforts compound over time when you stay consistent. Each day you maintain discipline, you build on the progress of the previous day, creating a powerful forward momentum that propels you closer to your objectives.

3. **Strengthening Willpower**: Discipline often requires resisting temptations or overcoming obstacles. Consistency helps strengthen your willpower. When you repeatedly make choices that align with your goals, you exercise your self-control muscles. Over time, this can enhance your ability to make disciplined decisions even in the face of temptation or adversity.

4. **Tracking Progress**: Consistency allows you to track your progress effectively. When you maintain a consistent routine, you have a clear baseline for measuring your ad-

vancement. This helps you assess what's working and what needs adjustment, allowing for more informed decision-making on your disciplined path.

5. **Building Trust and Reliability**: Consistency builds trust, not only with others but also with yourself. When you consistently follow through on your commitments and maintain discipline, you develop a reputation for reliability. This self-trust becomes a powerful motivator, reinforcing your belief that you can achieve your goals.

6. **Reducing Decision Fatigue**: Consistency reduces decision fatigue. When you establish consistent routines and habits, you eliminate the need to make repetitive choices about what to do next. This frees up mental energy and willpower for more critical decisions, enhancing your overall discipline.

7. **Long-Term Perspective**: Discipline often involves setting specific goals and priorities. Consistency ensures that you remain focused on these objectives and resist immediate gratification. It prevents you from becoming easily swayed by short-term distractions or temptations and reminds you that the journey towards your goals is a marathon, not a sprint.

8. **Overcoming Plateaus**: On any disciplined journey, you're likely to encounter plateaus or periods of slow progress. Consistency helps you push through these phases by reminding you to stay the course, even when immediate results are not apparent. It's during these times that small, consistent efforts accumulate and lead to significant results in the long run.

9. **Inspiring Others**: Consistency sets an example for others. Your disciplined lifestyle can inspire those around you, whether it's family, friends, or colleagues. By demonstrating the power of consistency, you may encourage others to pursue their goals with discipline.

10. **Reducing Stress**: Inconsistency often leads to chaos and stress. When you're consistent in your actions and routines, you create a sense of order and predictability in your life. This can reduce stress and anxiety.

Endnotes

1	John C. Maxwell Quotes. (n.d.). BrainyQuote.com. Retrieved October 28, 2023, from BrainyQuote.com Web site: https://www.brainyquote.com/quotes/john_c_maxwell_451127

2	Warren, R. (n.d.). Goodreads.com. Retrieved October 1, 2023, from Goodreads.com Website: https://www.goodreads.com/author/quotes/711.Rick_Warren

3	Merriam-Webster. (2023). Definition of "Arrogance". In Merriam-Webster.com. https://www.merriam-webster.com/dictionary/arrogance

4	Merriam-Webster. (2023). Definition of "Pride". In Merriam-Webster.com. https://www.merriam-webster.com/dictionary/pride

5	Johnson, C. (2003). Enron's Ethical Collapse: Lessons for Leadership Educators. Journal of Leadership Education, Vol. 2, Issue 1, Retrieved from https://journalofleadershiped.org/jole_articles/enrons-ethical-collapse-lessons-for-leadership-educators/

6	Berger, S., & Tausanovitch, A. (2018, July 30). Lessons From Watergate. Retrieved from https://www.americanprogress.org/article/lessons-from-watergate/

7	Levy, D. (2012, August 24). Lance Armstrong Let Pride and Hubris, Not Doping, Ruin His Legacy. Bleacher Report. Retrieved from https://bleacherreport.com/articles/1309680-lance-armstrong-let-pride-and-hubris-not-doping-ruin-his-legacy

8	Sayers, G., & Heinz, A. E. (1970). I am Third. Viking Press.

9	DePree, M. (1989). "The first responsibility of a leader is to define reality." In Leadership is an Art (p. 11). Doubleday.

10	Fleisher, Michael L. (2007). The Original Encyclopedia of Comic Book Heroes, Volume Three: Superman. DC Comics. p.88-90. ISBN 978-1-4012-1389-3.

11   Low, K. C. P., Ang, S. L., & Robertson, R. W. (2012). Gandhi and His Value of Humility. Leadership & Organizational Management Journal, Volume 2012 (Issue 3), 105-116. ISSN 2152-8675.

12   Luse, L. (2022, March 28). Nero: A Mother's Son. Memoria Press. Retrieved from https://www.memoriapress.com/articles/nero-a-mothers-son/

13   Drake, D. (2022, May 27). Career Insight: 5 Leadership Truths from Microsoft CEO Satya Nadella. Global Youth. Retrieved from https://globalyouth.wharton.upenn.edu/articles/career-insight/career-insight-5-leadership-truths-from-microsoft-ceo-satya-nadella/

14   Liedtke, M. (2023, May 27). As Elizabeth Holmes heads to prison for fraud, many puzzle over her motives. AP News. Retrieved from https://apnews.com/article/elizabeth-holmes-fraud-theranos-prison-silicon-valley-9552b17d0c03f81c71b53fb4a99446

15   Knowledge at Wharton Staff. (2012, October 2). Tylenol and the Legacy of J&J's James Burke. Retrieved from https://knowledge.wharton.upenn.edu/article/tylenol-and-the-legacy-of-jjs-james-burke/

16   Hayes, A. (2023, August 29). The Rise and Fall of WorldCom: Story of a Scandal. Investopedia. Retrieved from https://www.investopedia.com/terms/w/worldcom.asp

17   George Foreman Quotes. (n.d.). BrainyQuote.com. Retrieved October 28, 2023, from BrainyQuote.com Web site: https://www.brainyquote.com/quotes/george_foreman_613405

18   Congressional Medal of Honor Society. (n.d.). Freddie Stowers. Retrieved from https://www.cmohs.org/recipients/freddie-stowers

19   Cambridge University Press. (n.d.). Integrity. In Cambridge Dictionary. Retrieved from https://dictionary.cambridge.org/dictionary/english/integrity

20   Cambridge University Press. (n.d.). Character. In Cambridge Dictionary. Retrieved from https://dictionary.cambridge.org/dictionary/english/character

21	Kouzes, J., & Posner, B. (2011). Credibility. p. 8. Jossey--Bass.

22	Csorba, L. T. (2004). Trust: The One Thing That Makes or Breaks a Leader (p. xxiv). Thomas Nelson.

23	Birmingham Editorial Board. (2014, September 24). "With excessive force testimony staring him down, Birmingham Police Chief Roper doesn't blink". Birmingham News. Retrieved from https://www.al.com/opinion/2014/09/with_excessive-force_case_star.html

24	Gino, F., Ordóñez, L. D., & Welsh, D. (2014). "How Unethical Behavior Becomes Habit". Harvard Business Review. Retrieved from https://hbr.org/2014/09/how-unethical-behavior-becomes-habit

25	George, B. (2015). Discover Your True North. p. 118. John Wiley & Sons.

26	Rice, J. (n.d.). Good reads.com. Retrieved October 30, 2023, from Good reads.com Website: https://www.goodreads.com/quotes/197367-today-i-will-do-what-other-s-won-t-so-tomorrow-i

27	"The Torture Test: Timex Proves 'It Takes a Licking' ... for Over 60 Years." (n.d.). Retrieved from https://www.aaaa.org/timeline-event/torture-test-timex-proves-takes-licking-sixty--years/

28	Papies, E. K., Barsalou, L. W., Claassen, M. A., Davis, T., Farrar, S. T., Gauthier, E., Rodger, A., Tatar, B., Wehbe, L. H., & Werner, J. (2022). Grounding motivation for behavior change. In B. Gawronski (Ed.), Advances in Experimental Social Psychology (Vol. 66, pp. 107-189). Academic Press. https://doi.org/10.1016/bs.aesp.2022.04.002

29	Collins, J. (2001). Good To Great. p.31. Random House Business Books.

30	Tinsley, J. (2022, May 6). For Allen Iverson, it was never just about 'practice': The unforgettable news conference was a long time in the making. Andscape. https://andscape.com/features/for-allen-iverson-it-was-never-just-about-practice/

31   Harris, L. (1989). I Can Begin Again [Recorded by Larnelle Harris]. On I Can Begin Again.

32   Leventhal, H., Singer, R., & Jones, S. (1965). Effects of fear and specificity of recommendation upon attitudes and behavior. Journal of Personality and Social Psychology, 2(1), 20.

33   Maxwell, J. (2015). Intentional Living. p. 42. New York, NY: Center Street.

34   Colin Powell Quotes. (n.d.). BrainyQuote.com. Retrieved October 28, 2023, from BrainyQuote.com Web site: https://www.brainyquote.com/quotes/colin_powell_138130

35   Air Force Memorial. (n.d.). Quote by General Daniel Chappie James

36   Collins, J. (2005). Good To Great and the Social Sectors: A Monograph to Accompany Good to Great (Why Business Thinking is not the Answer). p.14. Harper-Collins.

37   Helen Keller Quotes. (n.d.). BrainyQuote.com. Retrieved October 28, 2023, from BrainyQuote.com Web site: https://www.brainyquote.com/quotes/helen_keller_382259

38   August 7, 1990, President George H.W. Bush orders Operation Desert Shield." (n.d.). Retrieved from https://www.history.com/this-day-in-history/bush-orders-operation-desert-shield

39   9/11 Memorial & Museum. "Commemoration." 9/11 Memorial & Museum, https://www.911memorial.org/connect/commemoration

40   Bearak, Barry (September 13, 2001). "After The Attacks: The Afghans; Taliban Plead for Mercy to the Miserable in a Land of Nothing". The New York Times.

41   Sidney J. Harris Quotes. (n.d.) QuoteFancy.com. Retrieved October 7, 2023, from QuoteFancy.com Website: https://quotefancy.com/quote/757832/Sydney-J-Harris-Our-dilemma-is-that--we-hate-change-and-love-it-at-the-same-time-what-we

42   "Embrace." Dictionary.com, https://www.dictionary.com/browse/embrace.

43   Emerson, R. W. (n.d.). "The only person you are destined to become is the person you decide to be." Goodreads. Retrieved from https://www.goodreads.com/quotes/73656-the-only-person-you-are-destined-to-become-is-the

44   General CQ Brown's Accelerate Change or Lose strategy. (n.d.). Retrieved from https://www.airandspaceforces.com/app/uploads/2020/09/CSAF-22-Strategic-Approach-Accelerate-Change-or-Lose-31-Aug-2020.pdf

45   King, Martin Luther, Jr. "Letter from Birmingham Jail." Bates College, http://abacus.bates.edu/admin/offices/dos/mlk/letter.html.

46   U.S. Census of Population and Housing (1990). "Birmingham's Population, 1880–2000". Birmingham (Alabama) Public Library. Archived from the original on January 21, 2008. Retrieved March 13, 2008

47   Birmingham Civil Rights National Monument. (n.d.). Retrieved from http://npshistory.com/publications/bicr/index.htm

48   "The National Initiative for Building Community Trust and Justice." Trustandjustice.org, https://trustandjustice.org/about/mission.

49   Bridges, W. (2009). Managing Transitions: Making the Most of Change. Da Capo Press.

50   Rumelt, R. (2011). Good Strategy Bad Strategy: The Difference and Why It Matters. Profile Books.

51   Bohn, D. (2020, May 30). Google delays Android 11 beta announcement because of protests. The Verge. Retrieved from https://www.theverge.com/2020/5/30/21275399/google-delays-android-11-beta-announcement-protests-george-floyd

52   Ndukwe Kalu Quotes. (n.d.). Goodreads.com. Retrieved October 16, 2023, from Goodreads.com Website: https://www.goodreads.com/quotes/56602-the-things-you-do-for-yourself-are-gone-when-you

Author's Bio

A.C. Roper is a transformative leader whose impact spans local communities to the highest levels of national defense. A decorated Citizen-Soldier, he made history as the first African American Lieutenant General in U.S. Army Reserve history, retiring as Deputy Commander of U.S. Northern Command, where he oversaw homeland defense and disaster response. His distinguished 42-year military career and 33 years in law enforcement, including a decade as Birmingham's Chief of Police, shaped his expertise in leadership, crisis management, and strategic operations.  As the founder of A.C. Roper & Associates, he equips leaders and organizations through executive coaching and consulting. A sought-after keynote speaker, he has appeared on HBO, ESPN, and major media platforms, offering insights on leadership, resilience, and legacy. With degrees from Troy University, the University of Alabama, and the U.S. Army War College, as well as training at Harvard and the FBI National Academy, A.C. is deeply committed to developing leaders at every level. He and his wife, Edith, co-lead Rest in Grace Ministries and celebrate 40 years of marriage, cherishing their shared journey and the achievements of their two daughters.

www.ingramcontent.com/pod-product-compliance
Lightning Source LLC
Chambersburg PA
CBHW032045150426
43194CB00006B/426